12 ways
to turn your **PAIN** into
praise

12 ways
to turn your PAIN into
praise

Biblical Steps to
Wholeness in Christ

Linda Newton

Warner Press
Anderson, Indiana

Coordinator of Publishing & Creative Services
Church of God Ministries, Inc.
PO Box 2420
Anderson, IN 46018-2420
800-848-2464
www.chog.org

To purchase additional copies of this book, to inquire about distribution, and for all other sales-related matters, please contact:

Warner Press, Inc.
PO Box 2499
Anderson, IN 46018-2499
800-741-7721
www.warnerpress.org

"Donnetta Jean Jones" is a composite case study of several persons who have counseled with the author and is not intended to depict the experience of any actual individual, living or dead.

Cover design by Carolyn Frost
Text design by Carolyn Frost
Edited by Joseph D. Allison & Stephen R. Lewis

ISBN-13: 978-1-59317-316-6

Library of Congress Cataloging-in-Publication Data

Newton, Linda, 1954-
   Twelve ways to turn your pain into praise : biblical steps to wholeness in Christ / by Linda Newton.
        p.   cm.
   ISBN 978-1-59317-316-6 (pbk.)
   1. Pain--Religious aspects--Christianity. 2. Suffering--Religious aspects--Christianity. I. Title.
BV4909.N49 2008
248.8'6--dc22   2008005099

Printed in the United States of America.

08 09 10 11 12 13 / VP / 10 9 8 7 6 5 4 3 2 1

contents

chapter 1

Predicament: Donnetta Jean Jones

Her name was Donnetta Jean Jones, and she couldn't have weighed more than a hundred pounds soaking wet. She slipped past the secretary into my office that first time, apologizing to the furniture as she walked by, a diaper bag on one hip and a beautiful ten-month-old baby boy on the other. After spreading out a quilt and toys for the baby with meticulous care, she slid back onto the sofa, careful not to take up too much room. She hooked her long blond hair around her ear, and in a voice that was barely audible she unraveled her tale.

"I'm not sure where to start," she offered, biting the corner of her lip nervously.

Sensing her apprehension and wanting her to feel like this was a safe place to tell her story, I offered a reassuring smile. Then focusing all my attention on her, I made comfortable eye contact and suggested, "How about you just talk, and I'll sort it all out." Then I turned to a clean page in my note pad and grabbed a pen from the end table to validate that her words were important to me.

She smiled back in relief and started. "I spent last weekend at the women's retreat where you spoke. After I heard you, I thought, *This lady has been reading my e-mail. I think she can help me, and boy do I need help. My life is a royal mess,*" she confessed with her whole body. Continuing to bite her lip, she hesitated.

I nodded my head to indicate that I was listening and continued to focus, so she kept going. "Two months ago I left Charlie's dad," she shared as she reached out and stroked her son's blond ringlets, smiling at him as she spoke. He grinned from ear to ear and tried to stuff his entire toy skunk into his mouth all at once.

"He cheated on me," she said flatly as she turned her gaze from her cooing baby. Her gray-green eyes grew cold as she stared numbly past my head at a picture on the wall. "It wasn't the first time; it was just the first time that he wasn't able to convince me to stay with him after I'd caught him in another lie," she continued.

"How long were the two of you together?" I asked, probing for more information, wanting to see if she would register any emotion for all of the pain she was sharing.

"Eric and I got married six months after we met, when I found out I was pregnant. He was the first guy who ever said he loved me—and I believed him. The girl before me must have believed him too when he got her pregnant." Her voice, though soft, now dripped with sarcasm. "I don't know if she's the one who gave him an STD, but I know he shared that special present with me! I feel like such a fool."

"Where is Eric now?" I asked, matching her soft pitch to keep her opening up.

"I don't know. When I walked out, I wanted as far away from him as I could get. I had no place to go, so I moved in with my parents. That's been a nightmare of its own," she shared, barely bothering to get her breath. It was obvious she needed to dump some of her pent-up stress.

"My dad never listens. He comes through the door every evening barking orders like a German commandant. Then he parks himself in front of his guy shows and yells at anyone who disturbs him—including Charlie. He treats the remote with more respect than he treats us! He refuses to come to the table unless everything is perfect, meaning exactly like he wants it, but he would rather die than offer any help. 'That's women's work,' he says about everything, even taking out the trash. 'Men have to save themselves for the important stuff. They can't be troubled with the grunt work.' I can't believe he actually says that, or that my mom puts up with it."

"He acts so smug and holy, spouting stuff from the Bible while he's ordering my mom around the kitchen like she's his personal slave! Then he wonders why I won't go to church with him. He's made me hate church and Christians." She heaved a heavy sigh of relief, but I could tell she still had more emotional bags to unpack.

"Is it just Charlie and you living with your mom and dad?" I wanted to know more about her family system, her birth order, and anything else I could piece together about the hurt she had been through.

"Everyone else has already moved out of my parents' house. I'm the youngest, four boys and then me. I'm named Donnetta after my dad, because boys are more important than girls and he can use the Bible to prove it."

Dad was smug, difficult, and demanding, and so, she was sure, was God.

"My older brother Andy lives just two blocks from my parents. He's got three kids. He and his wife unload them on my mom all the time. That means they're under my feet and in my hair. They're way too rough around Charlie, but every time I say anything to my mom, she tells me how hard things are for Andy and Cynthia and how I need to have compassion for them. I just want to yell, 'What about compassion for me?'" All the emotion she'd been suppressing suddenly surfaced as her face flushed and tears sprang to her eyes. She slowed her pace and struggled to talk, and I leaned in so I wouldn't miss anything.

"It's hard for me to even look at my brother, Andy," she shared, tears now steadily streaming down her cheeks. "He molested me." Donnetta cast a glance my direction to see if she was being judged. I kept my gaze steady, nodding my head in favorable feedback.

"It started when I was nine and he was thirteen, and he kept it up until he was fifteen and got a girlfriend." By now she was crying hard, and I kept handing her tissues and nodding in support as she poured out her story. I fought the urge to hug and comfort her as she cried; I knew from past experience that the comfort might shut down the feelings that were finally beginning to flow. I've seen people-pleasers who were so afraid their tears were upsetting others around them, they would stop crying no matter how much they needed to unload their pain.

"My parents never knew. How could they be so clueless? How could they not suspect? But now I realize that my dad was busy focusing on himself and mom was busy making sure she didn't upset my dad, the God-Almighty-male! I blame my dad as much as I blame Andy." I could hear the anger beginning to mount in her voice. "He always said that boys were more important than girls, that God made women to meet the needs of the men. Then he would order us all to the living room, sit us all down, and preach us rabid sermonettes about how members of the weaker sex should know their place and how God punishes women who speak out because they're supposed to keep quiet. No wonder Andy was so whacked! I didn't even bother to tell my parents what he did. I knew my mother wouldn't do anything, and I was afraid my dad would find a way to make it my fault. Deep inside I already feared that it was."

My heart ached for this attractive girl who sat in front of me feeling used and used up at the ripe old age of twenty-two. Donnetta exhaled like she had just unloaded a heavy package she had been hauling around for far too long. Then a second surge of tears surfaced, and I handed her more tissues as she started in again.

"I try to pray, but it feels like my prayers just keep hitting the ceiling. I've lost count of the times I've asked God to get me out of this nuthouse." She blew her nose and resumed. "It wasn't always like this. I prayed all the time when I was in high school. Then one day when I was walking home, I found my cat lying in the middle of the road. Misty was my only friend in the world, and a car had obviously hit her. I rushed into the house crying and yelling for my dad. While I was calling for him, I actually thought, *Donnetta, why are you wasting your breath? He's never been there for you before!* But I was desperate. My dad was sitting at the kitchen table scowling at me. Do you know what he said?" Donnetta wasn't asking; she was telling and I was all ears.

"He said, 'God is punishing you for missing church to go on that band trip. He's got to teach you a lesson somehow.' He wouldn't even come out to help me move her mangled body from the middle of the road. I thought I would never stop crying that day. I was angry at dad for what he said, but I was frustrated with God too for being so hard to please." Then with defeated resignation she added, "Why does God always seem to be the guy who, when you ask for a chocolate chip muffin, gives you zucchini because it's good for you?"

What honesty! I thought. *This kind of vulnerability needs to be validated.* In a quiet, even tone I responded, "Whoa, girl, that's as real as I've heard anybody share in this office. Thank you for trusting me with your feelings. With that kind of gut-level honesty, I know where to begin. We have to start by taking your dad's face off of God!"

Her expression was one of relief and curiosity. Weighing her response carefully, I decided to press on. "It seems to me you've got the wrong guy. You're mad at the God your dad represented to you by his words and his actions. But that is not a picture of who God is. I'm going to show you what he's really like and how crazy he is about you. Yeah, you, girl, the person sitting in your seat!" A weary but relieved smile crept over Donnetta's face, and I continued, "And I have no doubt that he will show you how to trust him again, because he's going to heal your pain and restore you to wholeness—if you'll let him."

Donnetta Jean is not alone in her struggle. Many Christians hit hard times in their lives and find it difficult to muster the faith to keep believing. Some walk away from God. Others are too afraid of his wrath to bail out on Christianity all together, so they distance themselves and tell God to talk to the hand! They may continue in church, but they don't pursue him any more because they don't believe he is watching out for them. Then they face the difficult dilemma of desperately needing the God they can no longer trust.

Have you been there? When life delivered a truckload of pain and confusion to your front door, did you find yourself asking, "God are you there. Don't you care? How could you let this happen?" All the while Jesus is dying to let you know, well, he actually did die to let you know, how infinitely valuable you are to him. Listen to what the apostle Paul tells us in Romans 5:8. "But God put his love on the line for us by offering his Son in a sacrificial death while we were of no use whatever to him" (MSG). Verse ten goes on to say, "If, when we were at our worst, we were put on friendly terms with God by the sacrificial death of his Son, now that we are at our best, just think of how our lives will expand and deepen by means of his resurrection life!" I think the key phrase here is "we were put on friendly terms with God." But when tough times come, it's easy to feel condemnation, judgment, and wrath. I confess that, like Donnetta, in the early years of my Christian walk, I thought God was "Dirty Harry in the sky," his hand hovering above the "smite" button on his cosmic computer just waiting for me to mess up so I could make his eternity! Isn't a day like an eternity to God? The steps that served to restructure my understanding of how God really feels about me are the steps I employed to help Donnetta. Maybe they can help you too.

If we want to stop circling the drain in doubt, self-loathing, and fear of the future, we have to adjust our perspective. I honestly believe that before I shifted my paradigm, had God planted a burning bush by my front door to convince me of his love, I would have stamped out the fire and complained about the inconvenience. It took a long time for me to train myself to see God's love in my circumstances. But without that fundamental change, it didn't matter how much God intervened in my life to bring good, I wouldn't see it as such.

Every day, as the cup of life presents itself, we have a choice to make. We can choose to see the cup half empty, or we can choose to see it half full. That daily choice makes all the difference. We have all seen people from horrible life situations emerge triumphant; we've also seen individuals, with everything going for them, circle the drain. What's wrong in life is always available to every one of us; so is what's right. What we choose to focus on determines whether we will be happy, successful, productive, and fulfilled.

The first thing I asked Donnetta Jean to do was to focus on what was good in her life by writing a Blessed List. She had to list ten things that were right about her personally, about her situation, and about those around her. For folks like Donnetta who have spent so much time in the negative, figuring out the positive can be downright painful. But it's absolutely necessary. Focusing on "what's wrong with your world today," constantly playing that negative note, is a bad habit that has to be broken. It takes work and intentionality, and you might have to "fake it till you make it!" It takes embracing an attitude of gratitude every day. It takes constantly looking for things that are right, no matter how few they may be or how hard they are to ferret out. Donnetta complained about her assignment, but she was willing to do it because she was desperate for change in her life.

I understood her desperation. When you've had a lot of pain growing up, it takes a lot of concentration to believe that things will turn out OK. Your "truster," your ability to trust, may be broken. I have found that one of the best tools for getting people to feel safe enough to cooperate in their healing is to let them know they are not alone in their pain. Donnetta Jean knew I cared because she knew I had been where she was. She had heard my story, and I'd like to share it with you. But first, try this Truster Reconstructor. What have you got to lose except a bad habit? How desperate for change are you?

Truster Reconstructor

Write a copious and thorough **Blessed List.** List everything that is a blessing to you right now, everything that is good about you, your environment, those around you. No matter how hard it is to find, seek what is good and write it down. List everything from "I can grow fingernails" to "I am blessed to be born in a free country," and everything in between.

chapter 2

Perspective: Honey, Let Me Tell Ya

Whenever my favorite Southern aunt would tell a story, whether it was how to make the the best ambrosia or where the doghouse ended up after the last hurricane, she always started with, "Well, honey, let me tell ya…," and then narrated her tale. The account of my damaged "truster" isn't nearly as entertaining as Aunt Muriel's antics, but, well, honey, let me tell ya.

I wish I could say that growing up in the deep South, we spent happy hours saying, "Yes, ma'am" and "No, sir" and "Good night, John-Boy." But nothing could be further from the truth. In reality, I was ten years old before I realized that God's last name wasn't *Damn!*

My daddy took off when I was five, leaving my seven-year-old brother, my twin sister and me, and mama still pregnant with my baby brother. Raising four kids alone brought out the worst in my mother, and she had no problem taking out her rage and resentment on us. She became abusive with a bust-your-lip, black-your-eye kind of punishment. It was the kind of pain that stings your face for a while but sears your soul for a lifetime. Life in that broken-down, eight-hundred-square-foot monument to deferred maintenance we called a house was miserable. It was easy to see why my daddy left. I wanted to go too, but I was five. Where could I go? On those hot, sticky Southern summer nights, I'd crawl up into the mimosa trees in my front yard, watch the lightnin' bugs, listen to a train passing on the railroad, and whisper to that whistling train to take me away to anywhere—anywhere but here.

Mama waited tables during the dinner shift at a local restaurant and spent the rest of her time trying to escape her unhappy fate by sleeping. We tiptoed around like mice to avoid the wrath we faced if we should, God forbid, wake her up. With the only parent in the house either working or napping, we became the kind of kids about whom respectable Southern ladies wearing beads and beehives would say while sipping sweet tea, "They just ain't had no raisin'." And they were right. We spent a lot of our time out in the yard running wild.

Most of my mother's parenting consisted of shaming and screaming, pretty much at the same time. When she was awake, she would stand with her hands on her hips—all 250 pounds of her on a five-foot-four-inch frame—behind the screen door yelling, "You kids are drivin' me crazy. You're really gonna get it." We had a hard time trying to decipher what caused her ire from one moment to the next. It was crazy-making. You could hurl obscenities to one of the neighbors at the top of your lungs in the afternoon and go unpunished. But that night, you could spill your milk at the table and get beat with a belt until the welts drew blood. (You know how folks say, "Don't cry over spilled milk." I cried a lot over spilled milk.)

Life seemed so miserable that I was crying myself to sleep about something nearly every night. And if it wasn't me, it was my sister. I would reach out in the darkness, pat my sobbing twin, and whisper, "It's going to be OK," but I didn't believe it because it never got better. I felt lonely, lost, and utterly unlovable.

Once when I was playing with a neighbor girl, Susan Kelly, she asked for a drink of water so I gave her one. The next day Susan's mother called about the car pool and said Susan had woken up with the mumps. My mom went into a rage. She kept hitting me in the face until my lip split and my right eye wouldn't open. As I cowered with a mouth full of blood, I heard her yelling, "Look what you've done, you G** d*** idiot. Now all you kids are gonna get the mumps and miss school for weeks." Ironically, we didn't miss any school because of the mumps, but I did miss school waiting for the bruises on my face to fade. I could never figure out what I did to make my mother so angry with me all the time, but I knew it must be bad. I knew *I* must be bad. I believed everything she said; after all, she was my mother.

Being a fatherless family in the 1960s made us different. Most people seemed leery of "those kids from that broken home." So you can imagine our surprise when Maude Gober, a neighbor from across the street braved the no-man's-land of our front yard and invited our family to church. She brought cupcakes. I thought, *Chocolate! I'm in.* But knowing my mother wasn't much for religion, I really didn't think the idea would fly. I couldn't believe my ears when she told the neighbor lady that she would have us kids ready and waiting the following Sunday. I reckon Mama thought she could wreak retribution on those "holy-rollin' hypocrites," as she was fond of calling them, by sending her reprobate children to church. Curiously, that wasn't how those church people felt at all. They didn't treat me like the plague. They treated me like a treasure. It seemed surreal.

Mrs. Gray, my Sunday school teacher, took interest in me the very first day. She found out where I lived and took it upon herself to make sure I had a ride when Mrs. Gober couldn't pick me up. Every week she would show up and teach a handful of us kids a Bible lesson she had obviously spent a lot of time preparing. I couldn't quite figure out what was in it for her, but I told myself that I came for the cupcakes. Truth is, I showed up because this was the one place in the world where I felt cared about.

The sanctuary was quite an experience—so clean, peaceful, and reverent, completely unlike anything in my everyday world. I can still remember sitting in that hard maple pew in that little country church and listening to that deep-voiced, pulpit-pounding preacher talk about "getting saved." As a nine- or ten-year-old kid, I couldn't for the life of me figure out who was drowning! It only took a few Sundays to figure out that it was me. I was drowning in a sea of pain, loneliness, and plain old separation from God.

Every Sunday that preacher was faithful to give an altar call, and every Sunday I would grip the pew in front of me until my knuckles turned white, tears streaming down my face because I wanted to go forward. I wanted to give my heart to Christ, but I just couldn't. Nothing would ignite my mother's wrath more than if I "got religion." And you know what they say, "If Mama ain't happy, ain't nobody happy." In our house, that wasn't a humorous maxim; it was a mandate. I wasn't sure what my brother would do if I became one of those "religious freaks." I didn't know how my twin sister would react, and I needed her. So week after week I would come to church and feel God tugging on my heart. I wanted to ask Jesus to be my personal Savior. I wanted my sins forgiven. I wanted salvation. But I needed my family's approval more.

All through the week, I would think about the pastor's words. He said that Christ wanted me, that he would bring peace and joy to my life. *How could that be?* I thought. *My mom doesn't even want me.* At least it felt that way. I used to pray that nothing bad would happen to me until I could figure this whole thing out. I fantasized that if I was suddenly stalled on a railroad track, I would quickly pray, "God save me!" and he would. Or if I was falling off a tall building, I would whisk off a prayer, "Jesus save me," and that would take care of things. (Give me a break. I was only ten years old!)

Time passed and I said no to God so many times that I couldn't feel his nudge anymore. Mrs. Gray would tell us that Jesus was a gentleman and that he was not going to force his way into our lives. He had to be asked. That is something I lacked the gumption to do. Instead, I moved into junior high and quickly grew too cool for school, much less for church. So I stopped going. I turned my back on God, but he didn't turn his back on me.

Not long after I left, that little church hired a youth pastor, and of all the places in that town that he could have lived, where do you think the Lord set him? Right down the street from me. I will never forget the first day Richard Smith showed up on my front porch to invite my sister and me back to church. He had a grin so broad you could play chopsticks on his front teeth! *What in this pathetic world would anybody have to be so happy about?* I asked myself as I tried to think of a way to get rid of him. I didn't want to go back to church and cry any more. I was done with that. But Richard kept showing up. He said he would pick us up in the church bus and bring us back home the minute church was over. *I'll give him one thing, he's persistent,* I marveled. *I would have given up on me a long time ago.*

Not Richard! He drove an orange Volkswagen bug. To go anywhere in town, he had to pass our house to get to the main road. Every time he would drive by, he'd honk that shrill little VW horn. "There he is again," I'd say to my sister Beverly. We were downright rude to the man, but he kept coming, kept smiling, and kept inviting us to church. "We're gonna have to go to church just to get rid of this guy," I informed Bev.

Fortunately for us, relentless Richard grew more creative in his invitations. One Saturday afternoon, he showed up on our doorstep with a cute guy from the youth group. That was better than Mrs. Gober's chocolate cupcakes! I figured I might as well go to church. My life was already a mess, so what did I have to lose anyway?

The very next Sunday, Bev and I climbed into the church bus and headed up the road. The minute I sat down in that Sunday school classroom and heard those high-school and junior-high young people in a discussion, I wondered who'd given them the keys to my diary.

The difference between them and me was that they had answers. All I had was questions. Dennis Jr. stood up, a handsome, blonde high-schooler, and talked about how he prayed for strength to turn down the kids in the hallway offering him drugs. Then one of the Ledbetter sisters, a heavy-set girl, shared about the loneliness she felt and how Jesus befriended her and eased her pain. I walked out of that room saying, *They have what I want!* But I wasn't saying it out loud—yet.

As I walked back into the sanctuary that day, it didn't feel foreign. It felt safe. I sat down in the freshly polished maple pew, rubbing my hand over the smooth wood as I slid across. I savored the slight musty smell that I remembered from being there before. It gave me comfort. As the music enveloped me, I became aware of just what a sanctuary this sanctuary had been for me and realized I missed it.

It was the Sunday of the Arab and Israeli Six-Day War, and that same deep-voiced, pulpit-pounding preacher, Pastor Dennis Miller, stood behind the podium. Reverend Miller, as we always called him, was a large man with a ready smile that constantly conveyed his love for people. But he didn't let his soft heart hold him back from speaking the truth so that we could all do "bidness" with God (or business, if you aren't from the South). He'd get so enthusiastically wrapped up in what he was saying that before long, he was yelling! On this day, I forgot to strategically sit at least three pews back, because he would spit when he got wound up. This time I didn't care. He was saying what I needed to hear.

"As we look at the political landscape, times are scary," he shared with stern conviction. "Jesus could come back at any time, and the eternal question I have for you in this service today is, 'Are you ready for that trumpet to sound?'" He stopped only long enough to mop his forehead with a handkerchief. Then he drew a long breath and headed straight for it again. "These are the end times, and Jesus is calling all of us to him. What will be *your* answer to him today?" I felt like he was preaching just to me. "You will spend eternity somewhere, either in the lake of fire, where there is weeping and gnashing of teeth, or in heaven, where Jesus will wipe the tears from your eyes for eternity. But God gives you the free will to choose. Without Jesus, you won't make it to heaven. In John 14:6, Jesus tells us, 'I am the way and the truth and the life. No one,'" He pounded the pulpit as he repeated the last line, "I said, 'no one comes to the Father except through me.'"

I didn't know the way, but I was desperate to find the truth, and I certainly needed to get a life. So when that passionate pastor gave his invitation, I couldn't get out of my seat fast enough. I made my way down the aisle of that little country church, fell on that altar, and felt loved for the first time in my life! All I could say between my heartfelt sobs was, "I'm sorry, Lord. I'm sorry." I wept tears of pain onto that altar. I bawled for the loss of the love in my family. I shed tears of regret that I didn't say yes to Christ sooner. I cried tears of joy over the amazing acceptance I felt in the arms of Jesus. Suddenly, I was stabbed awake by reality. *Where is Bev?* I wondered. Then I saw her—a few spaces from me, praying the prayer of salvation at the altar too. We became more than sisters that day; we became fellow soldiers in a war, and we had no way of knowing at that time what battles we would face.

My eyes well up with tears even now as I reflect on God's amazing grace to me so long ago. While I felt so grateful for God's gift of salvation, my faith to trust him for everyday life was fragile. The people in my life had not been very dependable, so relying on God to come through was foreign to me. Then I discovered it, a verse tucked away in the Old Testament. I had been reading my devotions out of the New Testament, feeling like all those words written before Christ were for sages and scholars. But I believe this verse in Jeremiah 29:11 was expressly written for people like me: "'For I know the plans that I have for you,' declares the Lord, 'plans for welfare and not calamity to give you a future and a hope'" (NASB). My perspective on life was full of calamity, but God's perspective saw welfare, so I decided to adopt his.

That decision solidified my first step toward repairing my broken "truster." It was to *choose* to view life from God's perspective.

The importance of a person's viewpoint was brought home to me in an interview I saw. The host talked with two World War II soldiers who had participated in the D-day invasion. The first man was part of the army, the land troops transported onto the beach from destroyers. "The enemy was ready for us," he related. "Somebody must have tipped them off. Henderson boats deposited hundreds of soldiers onto the beach, and as soon as they reached the shore, they were mowed down by the enemy." All these years later, his face still betrayed the fear he felt facing the Germans that day. He said, "I looked around at all the carnage and thought, *We're gonna lose this thing.*"

The second soldier had been a member of the Army Air Corps, the predecessor of the United States Air Force. As he was flying in, he could see all the other planes surrounding him. Then he looked down and saw the USS *Thomas Jefferson* and other ships sending out hundreds of Henderson boats, which were depositing thousands of soldiers ready to fight onto the beach, and he said to himself, *We're gonna win this thing!*

The difference between the two men was their vantage point. The way we view things makes all the difference. Many times we're like the first soldier: we don't have the benefit of seeing the whole picture. That's when we anchor ourselves to God and trust him to work all things out for good.

If we find ourselves needing to shift to a positive perspective, as Donnetta did, we must be intentional about how we choose to see things every day. If we believe what God tells us in Jeremiah, then we can look for the welfare in our circumstances, even if calamity seems to be staring us in the face. That's why making a Blessed List works. It's not enough to just *think* of what is working in our lives; we have to take the time to write those things down. Writing an actual list programs the positive data into the hard drive of our minds and makes it a part of our internal dialogue. More importantly, it gives us something concrete to refer to. We need to review our list for at least fifteen minutes every day, recognize how blessed we really are, and realize how much worse off we could be. An old proverb says, "I complained because I had no shoes until I met a man who had no feet." No matter what our circumstances, things could always be worse!

That's why Paul tells us in Philippians 4:4, "Rejoice in the Lord always." Then he declares, "I will say it again: Rejoice!" The apostle instructs the Thessalonians (and us) to "be joyful always; pray continually; give thanks in all circumstances, for this is God's will for you in Christ Jesus" (1 Thess 5:16–17).

The scripture doesn't tell us to rejoice *for* all things but rather to rejoice *in* all things. I couldn't say, "Thank you, God, for my cruel and abusive mother." But I learned to say, "Thank you, God, for being my comfort in my miserable home." As I continued to praise him despite my circumstances, I recognized that I could thank God for a church that became a fallout shelter for my shell-shocked soul. I also had sweet Christian girls at school who blessed me with their friendship. My youth pastor was there to answer any of my questions about God, no matter how many or how lame they were. I realized I had a lot that was good in my life.

Donnetta really wanted to move past her negativity and doubt, so she sat down with a cup of tea and took an hour (which wasn't easy to find with a ten-month-old) to write down her blessings.

Now it's your turn. Do this for yourself. Don't hold back. List everything that is positive about you, from your thick hair to your common sense. Then mark down what is right about your family, your friends, your house, your spouse, your cat, and even your car! Leave no stone of thankfulness unturned. All that you have been given will surprise you, even if you are currently enduring some pretty challenging circumstances.

Truster Reconstructor

Take fifteen minutes each day to read, reflect on, and add to your Blessed List. Call it your **Faithful Fifteen**, because as you reflect on what is right in your life, you'll realize that things are better than you thought they were. Then you'll understand just how faithful God has really been to you and you can begin to trust him again. If you can't find time the first thing in the morning, then do it the same time each day and schedule everything else around it. Clear your head and begin to see your cup half full, not half empty, and watch your perspective change.

chapter 3

Power: I Got a Rock

Donnetta Jean rushed through my office door, pushed past my wing-back chair, and plopped down on the plaid sofa sitting against the wall. She whipped off the blanket she had draped around Charlie to keep him cozy in the brisk autumn air. "Look at this adorable outfit!" she said enthusiastically as she showed off her baby boy, clad in a train conductor's outfit, complete with hat, overalls, and bandana. I didn't know she was capable of this much enthusiasm.

"My cousin Annabel, who I haven't seen in years, called my mom last weekend. She was coming up to see my grandmother, and she asked about Charlie. Annabel has an eighteen-month-old boy and wanted to know if I could use any of the clothes he had outgrown. Can you believe that?" she asked, her eyes sparkling. "Of course my mom said yes. My cousin dropped off eight grocery bags full of clothes that will keep Charlie stylin' until the middle of next year! Some of the outfits haven't even been worn. And yes, I wrote that down on my Blessed List," she quickly added with a grin before I could suggest it.

"He looks like an advertisement for Oshkosh B'Gosh!" I gushed. "I can't believe he hasn't tried to pull his hat off. He must know just how cute he looks."

"I've been taking my Faithful Fifteen minutes to focus on my Blessed List like we talked about," continued Donnetta in that same vein of enthusiasm. "I believe it's helping me to feel better about myself, about getting married and divorced in ten months time, and even about having a baby so young. The good seems to outweigh the bad. But no matter how many things seem to be getting better in my life, my dad just keeps getting worse." Her high spirits faded as she talked about her father.

"You won't believe what he did this weekend. While Annabel and I were chatting and sorting through the baby clothes, my dad saunters in and comments, 'It's a good thing your cousin likes you enough to bring you her baby's castoffs. Without a husband or a job, you would have to earn clothes money standing in the middle of the highway with a cardboard sign.' Then he laughs that nasty arrogant cackle that he uses when he's putting someone down.

"I didn't react at first because I was so stunned that he would make such a blatantly cruel statement." Angry tears sprang to her bright green eyes. "When his words finally soaked in, I was devastated. In one fell swoop, my dad managed to make me feel like a loser, a burden, and a whore. The look on my cousin's face told me she was embarrassed for me, but also angry and hurt. He had insulted her too by implying that she didn't care enough to bring the baby some new clothes. I didn't want to make her feel any more uncomfortable, so I bit my tongue until I nearly drew blood, sucking back the tears."

I was glad she wasn't sucking them back now. She had moved from the presenting issue of anger to the underlying issue of her emotional pain. Now that we were down to the real issue, God could do some real healing.

Unfortunately, a lot of people feel just like Donnetta Jean because they have been wounded by uncaring parents. I knew exactly what she was experiencing, and regrettably, maybe you do too. Whenever I see folks like us, I think of the story Jesus told in Matthew 7. He was trying to explain to a group of people the all-encompassing favor God has for his children. To do that, he chose the most obvious example of unconditional love he had available—the parent–child relationship. "Which of you, if his son asks for bread, will give him a stone? Or if he asks for a fish, will give him a snake?" (Matt 7:9–10). If Jesus had employed the vernacular of my teenage daughter, he would have finished with, "Duh!"

Many of us feel like Charlie Brown from the TV special *It's the Great Pumpkin, Charlie Brown*. As he was trick-or-treating with his friends, going from one door to the next, Lucy crowed, "I got candy." Linus beamed, " I got gum." But Charlie Brown moaned, "I got a rock!" With each new door they knocked on, the outcome was the same. The other kids got candy or gum, but over and over again, Charlie Brown just got a rock.

God set the human family in place so that parents could pave the way for their children to understand the relationship of unconditional love and acceptance he has to offer them. Yet parents who are cruel, unaccepting, demanding, self-centered, or unsupportive train their children to feel like Charlie Brown when he muttered, "I got a rock." God expects our parents to love us. When they choose not to or they aren't able to, he is as disappointed as we are. However (and there is always a divine "however"), God can take that rock that we've been given and polish it into a precious diamond—if we let him. When we let him do that, his power transforms us.

Accessing his power is simple, but it's not easy. Often, those who should support us tell us instead that we aren't good, smart, pretty, or productive enough to make it in life. That is a lie of the Devil. Jesus warns us in John 10:10, "The thief comes only to steal and kill and destroy; I have come that they might have life, and have it to the full." We access God's abundant life when we believe his Word and accept his divine opinion of us. When Satan whispers in your ear that you're flawed and worthless, you can respond to his lies with the promise of 2 Corinthians 12:9: "My grace is sufficient for you, for my power is made perfect in weakness." It worked for the apostle Paul.

When the Enemy says, "God is so sick of your screwing up that he doesn't want you anymore," you can embrace the truth of Psalm 145:8–9: "The LORD is gracious and compassionate, slow to anger and rich in love. The LORD is good to all; he has compassion on all he has made."

Satan says, "You're a loser and you're never going to get it right, so why don't you give up now?" You can combat that lie with this truth:

"My God will meet all your needs according to his glorious riches in Christ Jesus" (Phil 4:19). God's Word has the power to transform us if we let it.

In my counseling office, I deal with many people who can intellectually acknowledge that God loves them. After all, doesn't John 3:16 say that? But the information fails to make the twelve-inch journey from their heads to their hearts. So one evening, I sat down at the computer and filled a page with scriptures that stopped me from circling the drain of despair and reminded me that Jesus loved me, warts and all. I left out some of the personal pronouns so that people reading these passages could insert their own names and take ownership of God's truth. I titled it "Jesus Loves Me, This I Know?" My goal is that by the time a person finishes with this exercise, they will answer this question for eternity. These verses tell us truth about who we are in Christ, releasing us from the negative thinking of self-doubt. Focusing on his Word puts us in touch with the truth that sets us free.

That's what Donnetta Jean needed, but first she had some unfinished business. Before she could embrace God's view of her, she had to let go of her dad's.

"No matter what I do, it's never enough. I feel like I reach out my hand, and instead of it being embraced and nurtured, I keep drawing back a nub," Donnetta lamented.

"I know. You're fired!" I remarked, catching her off guard.

"I'm what?" she asked with surprise as she looked up from the mountain of tissue she was holding.

"You're fired from needing your father's acceptance and approval. In fact, you're firing him from the dad role," I informed her with confident authority.

"What do you mean?"

"It's time to replace him. Let's face it, girl, he has never been good at giving you what you need emotionally—but Jesus is. So you are going to fire your dad and embrace Jesus as your new father. Paul said in Romans 8:15–16, 'For you did not receive a spirit that makes you a slave again to fear, but you received the Spirit of sonship. And by him we cry, "Abba Father.'" That means 'daddy' in the original language, and that's the kind of relationship he's longing to have with you. Firing dad doesn't mean you have to hate your father or tell him off. Ironically, you end up honoring him more.

"Here's what that looks like: When your emotional needs go unmet and your tank is empty, you will be further disappointed by your dad's constant condemnation. You disdain him for that condemnation and then feel guilty for your contempt. That is one destructive drain you don't want to circle."

"Tell me about it. I've been living there for twenty years!" she blurted.

"However, when you let Jesus become your daddy and allow yourself to feel a love so complete that he would give his very life for you, your emotional tank is full. It doesn't matter what your biological dad does or says because he's not in the daddy role anymore. You don't need his approval or admiration; the Creator of the universe provides it for you."

Donnetta sat quietly, processing all she was hearing.

"If my old pastor were here, he would have some sage Southern advice for you," I continued. "He was fond of saying, 'They can't get your goat unless they know where you keep him tied.'" Donnetta Jean laughed so deeply that she didn't bother to cover her mouth in the self-conscious way I had seen so many times before.

"Your dad gets your goat every time because you care so much about what he thinks of you. When you fire him from the dad role, you no longer have your goat tethered to his approval. You're going to tether your view of yourself to Jesus. Now when dad spews his negative attitude all over you with corrosive criticism, you say to yourself, *I play to an audience of one.* As long as your behavior aligns with the will and intentions of the Lord, you're good to go."

"That all sounds really good, but let's get real here," Donnetta protested. "I haven't made a healthy choice in years, and my world is a royal mess because of it. I don't have anything to offer God." From the vulnerable tone of Donnetta's voice, I knew that she hadn't opened up about these feelings before. She had shifted from focusing on the issues with her dad to her feelings about God. We were getting down to the deeper layers of pain and progressing closer to a real healing. "Why in all of creation would God want me?" she insisted.

"Donnetta, he wants you because you *are* his creation," I answered. "He doesn't love you for how you perform or what you produce. You're not a human *doing*, you are a human *being*. He truly loves you, warts and all! I'm going to prove that to you right now."

I explained that the next step to healing was to access the power of God found in his Word. "Paul calls Scripture 'the sword of the spirit' in Ephesians 6:18. Jesus himself, when he was tempted in the wilderness, used Scripture to combat Satan. And that same power is available to you." With that, I handed her the Jesus Sheet.

"What's this?"

"These are scriptures with blank spaces where the personal pronouns used to be. I want you to take a few minutes to write your name in the blank spaces. As you do that, I want you to take ownership of each scripture. Move slowly through the verse, meditate on each word, and let the meaning soak into your soul. Allow the power of God's Word to change you. Do you understand what I want you to do with the Jesus Sheet?"

The pensive expression on Donnetta's face made me wonder if she was following me. "I get what you mean about taking Dad's face off of God," she said finally, looking up from the page I had handed her. "If I could believe half of what these verses tell me, it would change how I felt about myself."

"That's right. God's Word gives you the power to let go of your dad, accept Christ as a caring parent, and stop listening to the lies of the Devil that rob you of your joy. Truth is, you really do *have* a rock, and it's far better than Charlie Brown's. Psalm 62:1–2 says, 'My soul finds rest in God alone; my salvation comes from him. He alone is my rock and my salvation; he is my fortress, I will never be shaken.'

"Embrace your Rock, Donnetta. Embrace his life-changing power."

Truster Reconstructor:

Complete your **Jesus Loves Me Sheet**. Place your name in the blank space provided in each verse. Read, ruminate on, and receive each verse as a message from God's heart to yours.

Employ the **Freeing Three**. Select three scripture promises. You can choose from the Jesus Sheet or find other favorites. Place them in three easy-to-see places—on the refrigerator, the mirror, your computer's screen saver, for example. Then read them three times a day for three weeks.

Jesus Loves Me, This I Know?

"Whoever touches _____ touches the apple of his [the LORD Almighty's] eye." (Zech 2:8b NIV)

"And he [God] knows the number of hairs on _____ 's head." (Luke 12:7 LB)

"Where can _____ go from your presence? If _____ goes up to the heavens, you are there; if I make my bed in the depths, you are there. If I rise on the wings of the dawn, if I settle on the far side of the sea, even there your hand will guide _____ , your right hand will hold me fast…For you created _____ 's inmost being; you knit me together in my mother's womb. I praise you because _____ is fearfully and wonderfully made. Your works are wonderful, I know that full well. My frame was not hidden from you when I was made in the secret place. When I was woven together in the depths of the earth, your eyes saw my unformed body. All the days ordained for _____ were written in your book before one of them came to be." (Ps 139:7–10, 13–16, adapted from NIV)

"The Lord is gracious and compassionate (to)
_____ , slow to anger and rich in love. The Lord
is good to _____ ; he has compassion on all he
has made…The Lord upholds all those who fall and lifts up all who
are bowed down…You [the Lord] open your hand and satisfy the
desires of every living thing." (Ps 145:8–9, 14, 16, adapted from NIV)

"I waited patiently for the Lord; he turned to
_____ and heard my cry. He lifted
_____ out of the slimy pit, out of the mud and
mire; he set _____ 's feet on a rock and gave
me a firm place to stand. He put a new song in my mouth, a hymn
of praise to our God." (Ps 40:1–3 NIV)

"The eternal God is _____ 's refuge, and underneath are his everlasting arms." (Deut 33:27 NIV)

"But God demonstrates his own love for _____
in this: While _____ was still a sinner, Christ
died for _____ ." (Rom 5:8, adapted from NIV)

"But he was pierced for _____ 's transgressions,
he was crushed for _____ 's iniquities; the punishment that brought us peace was upon him, and by his wounds
_____ is healed." (Is 53:5, adapted from NIV)

"And my God will meet all _____ 's needs ac-
cording to his glorious riches in Christ Jesus." (Phil 4:19 NIV)

"'My [God's] grace is sufficient for _____ , for my
power is made perfect in weakness.' Therefore, I will boast all the
more gladly about my weaknesses, so that Christ's power may rest
on _____ . That is why, for Christ's sake, I delight
in weaknesses, in insults, in hardships, in persecutions, in difficulties.
For when I am weak, then I am strong." (2 Cor 12:9–10 NIV)

chapter 4

Prayer: Present in His Presence

n his book *Purpose Driven Life,* Rick Warren states, "Of course, it is important to establish the habit of a daily devotional time with God, but he wants more than an appointment in your schedule. He wants to be included in *every* activity, every conversation, every problem, and even every thought."[1] We have the incredible gift of communicating with the Almighty all day long, but we often find that life gets in the way.

"I've been reading the scriptures I picked out from the Jesus Sheet you gave me in the last session," Donnetta reported, after showing me Charlie's new front teeth. "I chose 2 Corinthians 12:9–10 because it says that God's power is made perfect in my weakness, and boy, do I have a lot of weakness! I like Deuteronomy 33:27 because I need a refuge. When I wrote down the verses to put on the mirror in my bathroom, I put Jeremiah 29:11 on the list. That was one of the first verses you gave me. It's my favorite because it talks about welfare and not calamity, and it feels like all I've had is calamity; it's time for welfare, future, and hope. I was reading these three regularly like you said; then I woke a few days ago and I actually found myself praying. I'm embarrassed to say that hasn't happened in a very long time. It was cool while it lasted, but it didn't last long. I've really tried to concentrate and pray since then, but

---

1. Rick Warren, *Purpose Driven Life* (Grand Rapids, MI: Zondervan, 2002), 87.

my mind keeps wandering. I find myself worrying about how Charlie and I are going to make it or feeling guilty about being such a messed up person for so long."

"Donnetta Jean, I am so glad that you felt like praying. That tells me that your busted 'truster' is healing. Now, are you ready to be done with guilt and fretting?" I posed.

"I'm sick of being stuck. When I decided to get help, I said that I would do whatever it took. So I guess that means I'm ready," she conceded.

Now it's your turn. Are you ready to dump the baggage of guilt and shame you have been carrying around? First John 1:9 tells us, "If we confess our sins, he is faithful and just and will forgive us our sins and purify us from all unrighteousness." It doesn't say some unrighteousness; it says *all* unrighteousness. Psalm 103:12 says, "As far as the east is from the west, so far has he removed our transgressions from us." God informs us in Hebrews 8:12, "For I will forgive their wickedness and will remember their sins no more." After we confess our sins to the Lord, he is done with them.

However, often we sit down to pray and before we realize it, we are reliving our past offenses and poor choices. One woman informs God, "I can't possibly serve you, Lord, because of that lame decision I made." And he says, "What decision, sugar? I can't remember what you're referring to." Another earnestly prays, "Lord, I really want more of you in my life, but you don't want me because I made such a vile mistake." The Lord's response is, "That one is so far from my mind, I can't bring that to my recollection." If the Creator of the universe, the one who placed the planets in space, the designer of every intricate function of your complicated human body can forget about your confessed sin, then you owe it to yourself to do the same. At a Just Give Me Jesus rally, Anne Graham Lots told a crowd of nearly ten thousand people, "The Lord is faithful and just to forgive us. When we don't forgive ourselves, we're saying, 'Thank you for the forgiveness, Lord, but my standards are higher than yours.'"

Every day damaged people come through my office doors needing to get out of the guilt trap that is debilitating them. To help them, I share this story. Perhaps you will relate to the young man in this tale.

There was a little boy visiting his grandparents on their farm. He was given a slingshot to play with out in the woods. He practiced in the woods, but he could never hit the target. Getting a little discouraged, he headed back for dinner. As he was walking back, he saw Grandma's pet duck. Just out of impulse, he let the slingshot fly, hit the duck square in the head, and killed it. He was shocked and grieved. In a panic, he hid the dead duck in the woodpile, only to see his sister watching! Sally had seen it all, but she said nothing.

After lunch the next day Grandma said, "Sally, let's wash the dishes."

But Sally said, "Grandma, Johnny told me he wanted to help in the kitchen." Then she whispered to him, "Remember the duck?" So Johnny did the dishes.

Later that day, Grandpa asked if the children wanted to go fishing and Grandma said, "I'm sorry, but I need Sally to help make supper."

Sally just smiled and said," Well, that's all right, because Johnny told me he wanted to help." She whispered again, "Remember the duck?" So Sally went fishing and Johnny stayed to help.

After several days of doing both his chores and Sally's, Johnny couldn't stand it any longer. He went to Grandma and confessed that he had killed the duck.

Grandma knelt down, gave him a hug, and said, "Sweetheart, I know. You see, I was standing at the window and I saw the whole thing. But because I love you, I forgave you. I was just wondering how long you would let Sally make a slave of you."

Whatever it is that the Devil keeps throwing in your face (lying, cheating, doubt, fear, bad habits, hatred, anger, bitterness, or something else), you need to know that God was standing at the window and he saw the whole thing. He has seen your whole life. He wants you to know that he loves you and that if you will ask him, he will forgive you. He's just wondering how long you will let the Devil make a slave of you. The great thing about God is that when you ask for forgiveness, he not only forgives you, but he also forgets.

If you haven't confessed the baggage you feel guilty about to the Lord, do it right now. Pull out a pad and pen and prayerfully write down your confession. Ask the Lord to search you, just as the psalmist did: "Search me, O God, and know my heart; test me and know my anxious thoughts. See if there is any offensive way in me and lead me in the way everlasting" (Ps 139:23–24). Once you've poured out your sins onto the page, earnestly ask your heavenly Father to forgive you. Now, ceremonially destroy the paper. Put it through a paper shredder, toss it into a roaring fire in your fireplace, or tear it up into tiny pieces and throw it into the ocean or off a cliff. Then wrap up in the warm arms of God's forgiveness. The psalmist tells us, "Cast your cares on the Lord and he will sustain you" (Ps 55:22). In the original language, the word *sustain* means "to keep, receive, maintain, provide for, or to hold." The word used is the Hebrew word *kuwl*. It's pronounced "cool," and I definitely think it is!

When we remove the obstacles that keep us from connecting with Christ, we are ready for relationship. That happens when we stay connected with the Lord all day long. We have to be intentional about keeping the communication lines open. If I'm not careful, I find myself rattling off my morning prayers like items on a child's Christmas list. Then I say amen and run out to tackle the day. Then my day looks like this lady's.

Rebecca wakes up excited about the new day. She starts out with great intentions. She jumps into the shower and sends up a prayer for everyone—her kids, husband, her boss, his boss, her parents, the pastor, and even the neighbors to the north, who are never very friendly. Then she towels off, says amen, and sails into the day feeling pretty prayed up. Halfway to work her cell phone rings. It's her oldest, Susie. "Mom, Tommy missed the bus again."

"Put him on." Rebecca feels her temperature rise as she grips the steering wheel. "You are so busted, mister. No phone, no TV, and no video games. I can't believe you did this again. Is it so hard to get yourself ready in the morning? For crying out loud, you're almost ten. How hard can this be? You haven't heard the last of this. We will finish this later, young man!" Then she hangs up the phone just as her dejected son whimpers on the other end of the line.

Rebecca barely gains her composure as she pulls into the parking lot at work. Just as she exits the car, the door handle comes off in her hand. *Oh that's just great*, she grumbles to herself. *How many times have I had this into the repair shop? Those guys are such a bunch of rip-offs!* She shoves the handle into her purse, sucks back her mounting anger, and marches into work. As she enters the outer office, her mood worsens as she spots the secretary's desk empty—again. *How many days off do they give this woman? Fabulous, another day of her work and my work too.* The sarcasm doesn't make things better, but by now she's beyond the point of caring.

She rounds the corner to her cubicle and sees a note penned in black ink taped to the entrance. It's from her boss castigating her for not turning out the lights when she left work yesterday. *Oh, my gosh! I did forget. I can't deny it. I rushed out of here to get Susie to the orthodontist and I forgot to flip the switch. Now I've managed to tick off the administration. Well, I can kiss that raise goodbye.* Now feeling angry, guilty, and utterly frustrated, she rushes to the restroom for a meltdown and runs into Jenny, who works in the cubicle next to her. Jenny opens her mouth, stepping on Rebecca's last intact nerve, and Rebecca rips her head off! And Jenny's the gal she's been trying to get to church.

Rebecca thoroughly and earnestly laid her petitions before the Lord. But the day proved to have more anxiety than she could handle, and she found herself in desperate need of some peace. Let's rewind Rebecca's miserable day and try it with the Daily Dialogue.

Paul tells us in Philippians 4:6–7, "Do not be anxious about anything, but in everything, by prayer and petition, with thanksgiving, present your requests to God. And the peace of God, which transcends all understanding, will guard your hearts and your minds in Christ Jesus." And 1 Thessalonians 5:17 advises us to pray continually. So today Rebecca stays connected to the Lord all day long. She jumps into the shower and prays for everyone and the cat, but this time she doesn't say amen. She doesn't hang up the phone or turn off the computer. She stays online with the Lord.

She launches into her day. Halfway to work, she gets a call from her daughter informing her that once again Tommy has failed to catch the bus. Rebecca prays, "Dear Lord, please don't let me kill my son!" She takes a deep breath and pulls into the parking lot at work. As she's opening the door, the handle comes off in her hand. She immediately accesses the Lord's help not to say awful things about the repairman who continues to insist, "It's fixed. You must be letting your kids swing on it."

Rebecca heads through the door at work and notices a vacancy in the front office. This time she immediately prays for the sick secretary instead of deriding her. She's starting to feel some of that peace that Paul talks about in Philippians as she trades her anxiety for answers. She knows how to respond in life's situations because she's tuned in to God's frequency, and he's supplying all that she needs "according to his riches in glory in Christ Jesus" (Phil 4:19).

Rounding the corner, she spots the note from her boss. But constant communion with the Lord has been filling her tank all morning, so she isn't derailed by her manager's rebuke. Instead, she takes ownership of her part and purposes to do better in the future. When Jenny approaches, Rebecca is prayed up and presentable, and she doesn't wreck her Christian witness in the workplace!

I believe that the Daily Dialogue, that continued communication with the Lord, determines the difference between despondence and abundance. But you don't have to trust me. Try it for yourself. I'm fond of saying, "Then watch how God shows up." But the reality is that God is always there; we just aren't tuned in enough to notice. There are days he spends a lot of time tugging on your sleeve to get your attention, but if you're like me, you're too busy to focus as you barrel through life going ninety miles an hour on a dead-end street. But I challenge you to slow down long enough to look for his involvement in your daily routine—the parking space that opens up right in front of the store when you only have fifteen minutes to run in, the money that shows up unexpectedly at the moment of your greatest need, the peace you feel throughout a demanding day. He's anxious to show himself to you. Keep your heart focused, your ears open, and your eyes peeled.

Truster Reconstructor

Sit down with a pad and pen. Prayerfully write out your confessions, admit them to God, and then ceremonially destroy the paper—shred it, tear it up and throw it in the lake, burn it in a fireplace. Practice the **Daily Dialogue** and watch how it builds your trust in God's goodness.

chapter 5
People: We're in This Thing Together

Donnetta strolled in, her arms full of mother paraphernalia—diaper bag, car keys, purse, the bottle Charlie dropped on the way in—and Charlie. Running to assist her, I commented, "Isn't it amazing all the stuff you need just to take care of one little child?"

"You're not kidding. I feel like I need to drag along a U-Haul trailer for all of his things. Hopefully, I won't need any of it. I planned this appointment for his naptime. With any luck, he'll settle right down and sleep on this blanket." She sat Charlie down and he immediately embarked on all fours toward the electric heater on the wall. "No, Charlie," Donnetta snapped before he could reach his destination. He immediately sat down and looked at his mother as if awaiting further instructions.

"That was amazing!" I responded. "I raised three babies, and none of them came close to being that cooperative."

"People say I'm blessed," Donnetta remarked as she scooped Charlie up into her arms, stuck a pacifier into his eager mouth, and began rocking him to sleep.

"I'll say you are. Look at what a good boy he is." I spread Charlie's bright blue, bunny-covered blanket on to the floor next to the sofa. "Is this where you want him?" I inquired.

"That's great," she agreed. Then continuing her thought. "I'm starting to feel that I *am* blessed. Linda, you always say that God's got your back. Well, I'm beginning to believe he might have mine too."

A big smile spread over my face as I gestured for her to tell me more. "I'm all ears," I added.

"The day after I left here last week, Charlie started to run a fever and throw up. I took him in, and the doctor said he had an ear infection. In my mind, I immediately went to the worst-case scenario. One of my nephews had chronic ear infections and had to have tubes put in his ears. It cost my brother and his wife a small fortune, and then they had to keep water out of his ears, which was a major pain at bath time and with my parent's swimming pool. All I could think about was how hard it would be if Charlie developed problems. Then I remembered our conversation about casting our cares on the Lord. I kept saying in my head, *Casting is cool*, as I told myself to give it to God." We both laughed out loud at Donnetta's recollection of Psalm 55:22.

"Whatever works for you! I'm just thrilled you were able to recall it."

"Hey, not only did I remember it, I did what it said," Donnetta responded, enjoying our banter. "I asked God to take my worry. I saw myself laying all my motherly worries at Jesus' feet. It was hard to do, but it was easier than carrying it around with me and fretting about it for the rest of the week. By the next day, Charlie was so much better, and so was I."

"You process things well, Donnetta," I said with conviction. " We talk about things, and then you walk out of here and apply what we've discussed. That's because you're smart."

She lowered her head and dropped her eyes in disagreement. "Your body language is telling me you're uncomfortable with what I just said. What are you feeling?" I inquired.

"I'm not smart. My dad always talked about how smart the boys were and how mentally inferior women were. I assumed that meant Mom and me. He never indicated otherwise, even when I did well in school. I've never felt like I was intelligent, ever!"

"Well, I insist that you are. Many of the people who come into my office have a hard time applying the concepts we cover each week. You catch on easily because you're smart." I added emphasis to that last line.

"Donnetta, I want you to accept that compliment. Years ago I had a terrible time receiving good things people said about me. Then I heard my pastor say, 'Compliments are bouquets thrown from the hand of God.' When we don't take the compliments given to us, it's as though we are ripping the heads off the flowers God has given us, throwing them to the ground, and stomping on them. Compliments are God's way of telling us who we are. When we receive them, it builds our confidence in the qualities and gifts he's given us. But when we don't, we remain stymied and self-critical. I took my pastor's words to heart and stopped dismissing compliments some twenty years ago. In that time, God has had the opportunity to remake my self-esteem. Before that, I had to climb a ladder to look an ant in the eye.

"Do you remember when I asked you to do your Blessed List?" I asked. Donnetta nodded as she laid her slumbering son on the blanket I'd spread out for her. "I used the example 'I can grow fingernails.' because when I was first asked to compile a Blessed List, it was the only thing I could come up with after a half hour of thinking!"

"You're kidding!" Donnetta responded.

"I wish I was. I was truly circling the drain in sad and sorry self-loathing."

"That is so hard for me to believe."

"Thank God it's hard for me to believe too now. I hardly know that underconfident girl that was me so long ago," I informed her. "But I can recall those feelings as I'm talking with you. Having been there helps me know what you're feeling and what you need. You have to stop rejecting people's praise.

"Now, look me in the eye and respond with a legitimate and heartfelt thank you," I instructed. "This isn't just for me; it's for everyone who pays you a compliment. As you say the words, I want you to see yourself receiving a breathtaking bouquet from the Lord. Shove your face in the flowers and drink in their fragrance. Examine the exquisite beauty of each blossom. Now take the words that were offered in the compliment and see them permeating your being. Let them soak into your soul. Believe them. Recognize that they are God's words to you, affirming the good he created in you."

"That's hard to do," Donnetta said, blushing.

"I know. But it can change your life. Are you ready to give it a go?" She nodded her head and rolled her eyes, recognizing I wasn't going to stop until she did what I asked.

Trying very hard to maintain eye contact, she mustered, "Thank you, Linda."

"Thank you for what?" I was pushing and I knew it.

"For saying that I was smart," she said, trying to stifle a shy smile.

"And what else?"

"Give me a break, Linda," she pleaded, half laughing.

"I'll give you a break next week. Now what else?" I insisted.

"And for saying I know how to apply things well."

"Very good!" I praised her. "Now you can take that to the bank. And each time anyone praises you, I want you to hear those words coming from Jesus himself. Give him the opportunity to build your confidence by showing you who you are. By refusing to accept the compliments that have come your way all this time, you've missed many powerful confidence-building opportunities."

"Well, that could explain why my self-image is so trashed, couldn't it?"

"Ya think?" I quipped.

"It could also help to explain what happened at the drugstore this week. I went to get Charlie's prescription and saw a girl I went to high school with. We were in church youth group together for several years. We weren't close, but I liked her. She seemed like a real Christian. The weird part is that I panicked. I skulked all over the store to avoid running into her. I really couldn't figure out why. It was like I found her to be detestable, but I don't."

"Maybe you found yourself to be detestable," I suggested. She looked down and breathed a heavy sigh that told me I'd struck a nerve. "You feel like you have nothing to offer, and since people in your life have proven untrustworthy, why even bother to connect with anyone? They will probably just let you down. Everyone else has."

Tears of shame began to trickle down Donnetta's cheeks. I continued, "Trusting is hard because you have no foundation for trust, and that's not your fault. When you reached out for love and positive attention from dad—something that every child needs and every parent is supposed to provide—you got scorn and ridicule. When you reached for support from your mom, she bailed on you. They were your primary caretakers, so now that's been etched into your brain, wiring you to think you deserve it. The real truth that sets you free is this: You aren't flawed and detestable like you feel. And there are people out there who could prove to be trustworthy. Now that you move through your day connected to Christ, he can guide you to the ones you can trust. May I share some insights that will help you in making friends with them?"

"Bring it on," she said eagerly. Donnetta reached down to dry her tears on the corner of Charlie's blanket and said, "The only thing harder than trusting God is trusting people. The only people I have in my life right now are my parents, and they always get on my nerves. I know I'm not ready for a relationship with a guy. I've made too many mistakes to even think of going there. But it would be nice to have a girlfriend to go to lunch with, or another mother to call to discuss baby stuff. Heck, I would simply settle for conversation about anything but Bert and Ernie and Barney!"

We both laughed. "Well, roll up your sleeves and let's get to work."

What about you? Are you ready to learn some of the concepts that are critical to healthy connections with people? We really need the friendship of other Christians, so understanding how to maintain balanced relationships is essential for our personal growth and spiritual maturity. Here are three *C*s of healthy friendships:

- Let Confidence empower you.
- Don't let Comparison infect you.
- Don't get Conscripted by needy people.

Donnetta's lack of confidence kept her from so much of what God had for her. It caused her to settle for men who couldn't love her because she didn't feel like she deserved any better. It held her back from educational and vocational pursuits, and prevented her from something as simple as interacting with an old friend in the pharmacy. Like Donnetta Jean, our lack of confidence can limit us if we let it. However, if we allow the Lord to redefine us through the positive comments of the people he places in our lives, we will realize how much we have to offer.

James tells us, "Every good and perfect gift is from above, coming down from the Father of heavenly lights, who does not change like shifting shadows" (James 1:17). So what we seek is not actually confidence but rather "God-fidence." That's an understanding that God gets the credit for what is beneficial and capable in us. Such an attitude will cure both arrogance and insecurity. We no longer need to alienate others with our self-importance nor avoid them in our self-consciousness. We realize that it's not actually self-esteem we're seeking but "Jesus-esteem." When we embrace the Lord's view of ourselves, we're free to be comfortable in our own skin. God's opinion of us is revealed in his Word, through the compliments of other people, and through listening for his gentle whisper every day. It's possible to rest in the "God-fidence" of all he has given us and let it work for us in healthy friendships.

Comparison can be equally detrimental in our efforts to connect with other people. Donnetta Jean avoided people because, as she compared herself to those around her, she felt she was inferior to them. Everyone feels that way to some degree. But we waste valuable relationships when we continually weigh ourselves against others, because we don't know their whole story.

That point was made so clear when Angela came to see me. She was an exquisite Italian lady with a flawless olive complexion, big brown eyes, and cascades of auburn hair that was her best advertisement as a hairdresser. She was the talk of Topeka until she married Bart. Everyone knew the marriage wouldn't work, except for her. He was a demanding jealous drunk, but he had money and he said he'd take care of her. He told her he'd move her away from all of her hard work and build her a beautiful shop in their garage. Then she could do hair only when she wanted to. But Angela found out too late that it was just another way for him to control her every move.

"He did it again," she said, tears soaking her perfectly tanned cheeks. "He came home accusing me of cheating. Linda, he keeps me so busy cleaning the 'big beautiful house I worked so hard to buy for you' that I don't have time to cheat if I wanted to. I hate my life," she sobbed. "I want to be Elaine."

Her last statement didn't surprise me. Angela had mentioned Elaine quite a bit. Elaine had married Ernie, a millionaire who made sure everybody knew it. Ernie bought Elaine anything she wanted—a new Mustang, cultured pearls, and a fifty-thousand-dollar kitchen makeover. He had even purchased expensive colored contact lenses for her, even though her vision was perfect. Angela was always comparing her life to Elaine's, and that left her constantly feeling cheated.

After talking about her feelings, we explored a plan to get Angela's husband help with his drinking and restore some sanity to their relationship. As a new Christian, asking God for help with life issues was new to her, but she prayed with me that God would give her strength and wisdom in her marriage. She left that day with renewed vigor to seek the Lord every day for the help and hope she needed.

Guess who showed up at my door just one week later to the day? You guessed it—Elaine! But she didn't come for help, because she had already made up her mind about what needed to be done. She sobbed, "I can't take it any more. I don't care how much money my husband has, it doesn't give him the right to scream at me all the time. He yells at my boys too. Nothing they do pleases him. They are good boys and they don't deserve his abuse. I honestly think he hates them, and I can't figure out why. I'm ready to walk."

That day, I learned a valuable lesson about comparing ourselves with others. When Angela compared her life to Elaine's, she came up short, but only because she didn't know the real story. So now I don't compare myself to anybody, because I don't know what's really going on in another person's life. And neither do you. So you're fired from comparing. It's a huge waste of time. Spend your energy instead on reviewing your own Blessed List. When you do, you'll realize how good your life is in God.

The third helpful hint for healthy friendship is this: don't get conscripted or recruited by needy people. When we feel insecure, we often allow others to take advantage of us because of our deep need for acceptance and approval. We end up doing things for them that they need to do for themselves. In *Hiding from Love,* Dr. John Townsend explains, "I know many Christians whose lives are marked by fruitless attempts to take care of everyone in their lives as well as themselves."[1] He notes that Galatians 6:2 instructs us to take care of those around us: "Carry each other's burdens, and in this way you will fulfill the law of Christ." But verse 5 says, "Each one should carry his own load."

Dr. Townsend explains, "It's easy to be confused by this passage. Paul is discussing our responsibilities, and he seems to be saying, 'Take care of each other' (verse 2) and 'take care of yourself' (verse 5)… The Greek word for *burden* in verse 2 means 'overwhelming load.' It's the picture of a gigantic boulder crushing the back of a hurting person. Boulders represent deep, catastrophic losses in our lives—family and marital losses, financial devastation, physical illnesses, and so on… We are to look out for each other's boulders in the body of Christ. When one is 'crushed,' those of us with something to offer are to swarm around the hurt individual and love, support, and encourage her."[2]

The picture gets clearer as Townsend examines the word for *load* in verse 5. "It means 'knapsack.' It carries whatever daily essentials the hiker needs to make it through the day. A knapsack is an individual affair. It's only for the carrier. And each person is to carry his own."[3]

"Boundary conflicts happen when Hiker A tires of his knapsack and wants a free ride. Hiker B, wanting to be caring, takes it on. After a few miles, two things happen. First, Hiker A learns it's a lot of fun not to have to be responsible to pay his own rent, find a job, or take responsibility for his own happiness. Second, Hiker B shifts from love to resentment to bitterness as he takes on the impossible task of being responsible for another person's life."[4]

---

1. John Townsend, *Hiding from Love: How to Change the Withdrawal Patterns That Isolate and Imprison You,* 2nd ed (Grand Rapids, MI: Zondervan, 1996), 77.

2. Ibid., 77–78.

3. Ibid., 78.

4. Ibid.

Donnetta's poor self-esteem caused her to behave like Hiker B. It caused her to cave in to the demands of hurtful men—saying yes when she meant no, staying in relationships when she wasn't respected, and putting up with behavior that was against her values. As she grew in her understanding of how much God treasured her, she realized she was worth more than that. She could now hold off on dating until she knew herself better, which was a smart thing to do. Also, as she embarked on friendships with women, it was important for her to inventory her patterns in all of her relationships. She needed to seek involvement with healthy people and set firm boundaries from the start. Donnetta's assignment was to ask for the Lord's discernment in dealing with others. She asked the Lord to show her healthy folks who would give as much as they took and offer her inspiration and encouragement. And now Donnetta's assignment is yours too.

Truster Reconstructor

Muster the courage and energy to attend a church service this week. Introduce yourself to at least three people before you leave.

Make yourself go to one new event (e.g., MOPS, Ladies Night Out, Bible study) each week. Be open and available for conversation while you are there, even if you have to "fake it till you make it."

Mind the three Cs of **Caring Relationships.**

chapter 6

Patience: Locust Lunch

Donnetta dragged herself into my office. Dressed in tan pants, a white blouse, and a black blazer, she looked like quite the professional, but her body language let me know she wasn't feeling like one. "You're looking sharp," I noted, trying to lift her mood.

"I know I'm supposed to receive that bouquet," she commented, forcing a sideways smile, "but I'm too bummed. I left Charlie with my mom so I could go apply for low-cost housing. I've been everywhere, and the shortest waiting period is at least a ten months, and that's only for an apartment, not even a house. Linda, if I have to live with my parents that long, I'll be dead by the time something opens up!" We chuckled together. "I have to laugh to keep from crying."

"I know. This has got to be hard," I said, wanting to validate her feelings so she would continue to open up.

"I don't know how much more I can stand. My dad is driving me crazy. He came home two nights ago and went on a screaming rage about the cost of a dozen eggs. Charlie and I don't even eat eggs! But I had to sit there and 'be respectful' like my mother taught me. Linda, I try so hard to pray and find the peace-place; and one minute it works, but the next minute it doesn't. I'm being as obedient as I know how to be. I make myself go to church every week, and you know how hard that is for me. I try to read the Scriptures every day like you told me too. I just can't understand why God won't answer my prayers. I've prayed and prayed to find low-cost housing, I've searched all over two counties, but

I'm still living in this emotional ghetto with my parents. I can't see why God would have a problem with me being independent and getting Charlie and me away from the craziness. So why won't he answer my prayers? If God won't give me more than I can handle, I think he needs to take inventory!"

"I told you that your honesty would serve you well. This is one of those times. You've been very clear with me about your feelings. Now I want you to share all of this with the Lord. Don't let your disappointment distance you from him. I have found that I can vent my anger with God and it doesn't affect his sovereignty one iota. My temper tantrum doesn't push God off the throne. The truth is, Donnetta, he knows how you're feeling, so you may as well be honest and get it off your chest. It might help you to write it all down. Pour all your pain onto the page. If you're going to repair your broken 'truster,' you've got to give God a chance to prove himself trustworthy."

"It's just so hard to wait for answers. It's hard to believe God will come through," Donnetta complained.

"I've been in your shoes, girl—new to faith in God, not sure he heard my prayers, and unable to muster the trust to believe he would provide. That's when I ran across Joel 2:25, "I will restore to you the years the locust hath eaten" (KJV). This verse gives us the assurance that God is in the restoration business, but sometimes life seems like locust lunch. That's when your only hope is to hold on to God. Don't cringe in the devastation; claim the restoration. Trust God for it. He'll come through. He did for me."

Maybe you're in Donnetta's shoes today. You need patience as you wait for God to work things out, but past experience doesn't convince you that he will. If so, let me share with you the experience that I described to Donnetta that afternoon in my office.

Even after I gave my heart to the Lord, the locusts continued to gnaw away at my days. Most parents would be pleased to see their kids start going to church and behaving better. Not my mother. She did everything she could to discourage church attendance, but that just made me more determined to go. Worship was my lifeline, and I learned so much from the sermons that I lived for Sunday morning. Psalm 68:6 says, "God sets the lonely in families." The kind folks there became my family, bringing me to church, answering my questions, and praying for me whenever I needed it.

I tried my best to cooperate with my mother so that I wouldn't compound her anger. I diligently did what she asked, and since she worked evenings, that was a lot. I'd get up in the morning, go to school, come home, cook dinner, clean up the house, take care of my little brother, carve out time to do my homework, fall into bed at night, and get up and do it again. The minute I'd walk through the door from school, before I could put my books down, she would greet me with her hands on her hips barking orders like a marine drill sergeant: "You need to polish my shoes and press my uniform. Don't think you get to rest. I have to work, so you have to work. We don't get to take a break like other people," she would yell, still groggy from sleeping all day while I was at school. "Since that good-for-nothing father of yours walked out on us, that's how it is."

I would vacuum every room, scrub the toilets, mop the floors, and Mama would come in cussing because I missed a cobweb in the corner. No matter how much I accomplished, I never seemed to satisfy her. But I was a great codependent-in-training: I kept on trying. I joined the band, school clubs, and plays, and excelled at all of them, but none of my awards made her happy. She grew more angry, difficult, and demanding. I was doing the very best I could, and it still wasn't good enough. Life at home felt hopeless.

The one bright spot was a great group of girls that I connected with after I came to the Lord. My youth pastor spoke about the importance of choosing friends who made good choices, and I took his words to heart. I was blessed to find a handful of Christian girlfriends who didn't cuss, smoke, drink, or chew tobacco. In the South, that was no easy task. These gals were church-going, college-bound, Jesus-loving ladies. One of them, Janet Lindsey, was an articulate girl with cascades of bright red hair and endless freckles. Janet was always inviting me over to her house. Whenever I asked my mother if I could spend time at Janet's, her answer was always the same: "You don't get to be normal like other kids. I have to work, and you have to take care of the house."

"I promise I'll get all my work done ahead of time, and I'll work all weekend to make up for it. Please let me go," I begged. The more she said no, the more I pleaded. The way I figured it, she was lucky that I wanted to hang out with a kid who had Janet's qualities. My persistence paid off. She finally relented, but I couldn't spend the night. I had to be home no later six o'clock. I couldn't believe it! For one brief shining moment, I would get to be normal.

I met Janet in the hallway after seventh period. She drove me to her house in the powder blue compact that her parents purchased for her on her sixteenth birthday. We chatted the whole way, excited about getting to spend an afternoon visiting without being interrupted by school bells or hall monitors. Janet pulled into the driveway of her two-story yellow house with white shutters; it looked liked something out of *Southern Living* magazine. As I walked past the wrap-around porch full of potted red geraniums, Janet opened the beveled glass door and gave me a tour of this pristine place. After we sat chatting in the parlor for a half hour, her mother came in. She spoke five words that caused me to nearly fall off my chair.

She said to Janet, "Honey, how was your day?"

As Janet responded, I was on high alert. *Any minute now*, I thought, *Janet's mom is going to lose it. Then we'll see the real her. She'll start to scream at her daughter for leaving a towel in the washer or the cap off the toothpaste, or for not wiping off the kitchen counter.* But all Mrs. Lindsey said was, "Can I get ya'll some Coca-Colas? We've got some Tab too. Anybody want Tab?"

She brought our sodas, set them on the coffee table, and then busied herself, weaving in and out of the living room putting laundry away and looking at mail. For three hours, I watched her carefully, and for three hours that woman was nothing less than kind, courteous, and thoughtful.

I was silent on the drive home. Janet asked me several times if I was all right. I wasn't, but it wasn't her fault. I asked her to drop me off at the top of my road. After seeing her immaculate home, I didn't want her to see my white-trash house. I ran down the hill, threw open the front door, and fell on my bed. *Why, God? Why can't I have a Christian home like Janet's?* My words echoed into my pillow that night, but little did I know what God had in store.

At that dark time in my young life, I couldn't see that God was working all things for good like he promised in Romans 8:28. I didn't trust him for the future and hope he guaranteed in Jeremiah 29:11. I felt like a heaping pile of locust lunch.

Not long after that tearful night, my youth pastor shared at youth group from Proverbs 3:5–6, "Trust in the Lord with all your heart and lean not on your own understanding; in all your ways acknowledge him, and he will make your paths straight." I decided to trust God, and I claimed that verse every time life got crazy, which in my household was a lot. That promise gave me the patience to wait on God. Now, with the benefit of hindsight, I can understand that the Lord was working in my life even in the tough times—especially in the tough times.

Remember that Joel 2:25 says, "The Lord will restore the years the locust hath eaten" (kjv). Often after I learned this verse, I would quote it to myself as, "The Lord will replace the years the locusts have eaten." Then one summer I restored an antique oak library table from the 1850s that had been in my mother-in-law's possession. My husband wanted to use it as a desk in his office, so the project had special meaning. His mom had redecorated their home a dozen times. As a result, the once beautiful tiger-oak table was now covered in several coats of garish paint. To get to the real wood underneath, I had to slather on a caustic paint stripper that was so corrosive that I didn't dare let it touch my skin. I'd let it set a few minutes so the chemical could soften the paint, and then the hard work began—scraping layer after layer of scummy sludge off the desk. The old paint was stubborn; I had to apply countless coats of the corrosive chemical to the top of the desk and employ endless hours of elbow grease to restore the wood.

Before I even started on the ornate legs, I remembered a gorgeous roll-top desk I had seen at Costco just a few weeks before. More than once in the middle of that challenging task, I thought of backing the truck up to the loading dock at the store and hauling home a brand-new desk for my husband. But the antique table had sentimental value. The project meant too much for me to quit.

As I worked diligently on this project one afternoon, scraping and sanding for hours, I remembered the verse from Joel. As I recited it to myself in my usual way, using the word *replace* instead of *restore*, it hit me. Replacing this piece of furniture would be a picnic, but restoring the desk required messy, arduous, tenacious labor. The Lord doesn't promise to replace our wasted years; he promises to restore those years. That may require some laborious effort scraping the scum of pain and poor decisions from our souls. We have to scour off the sludge of bitterness and resentment and scrape off the layers of fear and doubt so that God can restore the beauty he intends for each of his children. In his book *Heaven,* Randy Alcorn states, "God always sees us in light of what he intended us to be, and he always seeks to *restore us* to that design."[1]

I believe that Jesus reaches diligently toward his children, but many times our ability to reach back is impeded by a big pile of emotional baggage heaped so high that we can't respond to his embrace. The process of unpacking the emotional bags full of damage that has been visited upon us or that we have visited upon others—and ourselves—requires considerable emotional elbow grease. But we can't give up because that transformation process means too much to us in terms of future peace and fulfillment. The Lord will be there every step of the way encouraging and empowering us to continue, but we will have to do the painful task of peeling off the layers of spiritual sludge and surrendering them to God. The process takes patience, and God will even help us with that. Philippians 2:13 states, " For it is God who works in you to will and to act according to his good purpose." Not only does God supply us with the tools for transformation, but he will also give us the desire to do so.

I finished restoring the library table, and it was a sight to behold! The rich buttery brown of the bare wood showed off the detailed grain of the tiger oak. The exquisite filigree on the legs that was barely noticeable before now displayed an intricate design.

I marvel at how that refinishing project mirrored my life in the toxic environment with my mother. There were times when just getting

---

1. Randy Alcorn, *Heaven* (Carol Stream, IL: Tyndale House, 2004), 88.

through the day was so difficult, I was tempted to give up on trusting God altogether. But I couldn't because it meant too much to me, so I kept going. And besides, where else would I turn for the help I needed to do life. I felt like Peter in the gospel of John. Jesus' teachings had become hard for folks to handle, so many "turned back and no longer followed him" (6:66). Jesus asked his disciples, "You do not want to leave too, do you?" (v. 67). It was Peter who answered, "Lord, to whom shall we go? You have the words of eternal life"(v. 68).

So I resolved to put one foot in front of the other and trust God to straighten out the path I was on. I purposed in my heart to be patient with his plan for me. The Lord came through for me in a mighty way, but before I tell you the amazing thing he had in store for me, we have to focus on where you are on the path. If your find yourself in God's waiting room wondering what to do, pause a moment for this Truster Reconstructor. Then pay close attention to the Lord's work in your life to restore the locust lunch.

Truster Reconstructor

What are you waiting on God to do in your life right now? Write down your request and leave space to record his response. Watch for his involvement in the little things of life everyday and write down these things in your journal as faith builders. Let them serve as a reminder that God is at work in your life every day.

chapter 7

Plan: Jesus in the Rearview Mirror

The sun sat low in the sky allowing the autumn light to bleed through the blinds. The wind rustled through the maple leaves just outside my office window providing a calming rhythm to my narrative. Donnetta had slipped comfortably down into the sofa and was listening intently. She barely blinked as I continued the story of how God's amazing plan unrolled in the midst of my pain.

"Jesus in the Rearview Mirror" was the sermon title I read as I opened the Sunday bulletin. In twenty plus years of marriage, I had grown used to being wowed by my husband. But this time he had the attention of the entire congregation with the unusual way he preached about God's plan for his people. Bruce explained that the view we have of what is happening around us as we cruise through life is often challenging, even frightening. From our viewpoint, looking through the windshield, we only see calamity, but all the while God is working. Later, when we look back over our lives, as we peer into the rearview mirror, we are able to see the future and the hope that God was weaving all along. But sometimes things get tough before they let up.

As a kid, I was always waiting for the other shoe to fall, and it did—on my head. Just when I thought things couldn't get worse, they did. My mother's spells of irrational anger grew more frequent and more severe. One evening as she was getting ready for work, she flew into a rage-filled fit that ended with her throwing my sister and me out. "I'm sick of this," she screamed. "I've had to do everything all these years. Call that louse of a man you call a father. It's his turn to step up, but I'll bet he won't even come and get you. Then you'll find out what a worthless jerk he really is. You need to be out of here when I get home."

I can't tell you how devastated I felt. As bad as my home was, it was all I knew. I loved my church, and I needed my Christian friends. Graduation was only a few months away, and I was on target to graduate as the salutatorian along with my friend Beth. She and I spent seventh period every day planning our speeches. Now that was shattered.

My dad showed up in the middle of the night to get us, but sometime in the hours before he arrived, my mother changed her mind. She then decided to call the police and tell them my dad had come to kidnap us. I stood trembling in front of the police car and told the policeman what really happened. Then he instructed my dad, "Get your daughters out of here." After one of the longest nights of my life, I found myself heading 350 miles away from all that was familiar to me.

I felt like God had forgotten me. How could he let this happen? One minute I was living in Tennessee and the next minute I was in North Carolina with a stepmother I had only met once and a little sister I barely knew existed. Didn't the Lord care about what I was going through? From where I sat, the view I had of life left me hopeless and scared.

Yet even in the midst of my faithless fear, God was working. Over the next few days while my dad looked into registering us for school, I tried to cope with all of the changes in my life. The little sister, Reneé, whom I had just met, was quite delighted with the prospect of having older sisters, especially twin sisters. She tried to be a helpful as possible, bringing us hangers for our clothes, sharing everything she knew as a junior higher about the high school we would attend, and educating us about all of the kids in the neighborhood. Then one morning as we were in the bathroom putting on make-up, she wandered in and perched herself on the counter to watch. "Can you put make-up on me?" she chirped.

Still shell-shocked from the stress, I welcomed the diversion. Besides, she was too cute to resist. "You're only twelve. Are you sure it's OK with your mom?" I questioned.

In record time, she bee-lined from the bathroom and then returned. Resuming her perch on the counter, she informed me that her mother had given the go-ahead. "I'm not going anywhere, so Mom says you can practice on me."

She sat patiently as I dusted her eyelids with color. Then out of what seemed to be nowhere, she piped up with a statement that was posed more as a question, "Daddy says ya'll go to church." I'm not sure how my dad knew, but he recognized that church had become an integral part of our lives over the past few years.

"Sure, we go to church," I responded.

She sat stalk-still as I mixed the perfect shade of bronze to accent the gold-flecks in her olive green eyes. "Daddy says ya'll like church?" she stated again like she was asking a question.

"Uh, huh," Bev replied, casting an inquisitive glance my direction and coating her hair with Aqua Net. "We like to go to church."

"Will you go to church with me?" she asked.

"We would love to go to church with you," I said.

Then, with her now shimmering eyes open wide, she asked the question she had been waiting to ask, "Are ya'll Christians?"

I dropped my blush brush. "Yes, are you a Christian?" I asked, looking into her freshly made-up eyes.

We spontaneously hugged each as we realized that nothing more needed to be said. There was so much we already knew about each other that defied words, so the three of us celebrated a pre-heaven reunion right there in that little bathroom. We made an agreement there and then to pray for our parents every day until they came to the Lord.

Making good on our pact, we dressed in our Sunday best and headed for church every week. We invited our parents any chance we got. With three of us asking, they didn't have much choice, so they started coming with us more often.

That fall, Bev and I headed cross-country to enroll at Azusa Pacific University. There, we had the opportunity to ask people to pray for our parents' salvation practically on a daily basis. When the school year was over, we flew home for the summer.

It was about that time that my dad found out that his younger brother had lung cancer. My father took the news pretty hard. We spent many weekends traveling from North Carolina to Georgia so that my dad could spend time with his brother. And we all watched week after week as cancer overtook Uncle Hugh.

An urgency to share the Lord with my uncle consumed me. I didn't want him to die without knowing that I would see him again in heaven. So I sat down after work one afternoon with a glass of sweet tea and penned him a letter. I explained to Uncle Hugh what Jesus meant to me, and I told him that if he would accept the Lord as his Savior, his brothers—and that included my dad—would too. I sealed the letter with the conviction that I had done what God wanted me to do and the hope that it would make a difference.

On our next visit several weeks later, Aunt Betty met us at the door. His condition had worsened. He was barely conscious and unable to speak. Aunt Betty asked to see me privately. I was surprised, given all of the activity going on, but she seemed intent on talking with me.

"Linda, he got your letter," she said with her soft Southern drawl as we crowded into the master bathroom close to her husband's bed. "You don't have to worry about your uncle, honey. The priest came and Hugh took care of business with the Lord. You will see him again." We hugged each other and cried both tears of sadness that he was fading and tears of joy that we would see him again.

A few weeks later, I was sitting next to my dad in the Episcopal church in Rome, Georgia, for my uncle's funeral. It was the first and only time I had ever seen my father cry. I hurt to see his sorrow. I wanted so badly to share the hope I had about Uncle Hugh with him. *Soon*, I heard the Lord whisper.

Several weeks passed. I was wrapped up in getting ready to go back to school when I felt a nudge from the Lord one morning to have a heart-to-heart talk with my dad. With our hectic schedules and only two days before my plane took off, I didn't know how that was going to happen. Then the phone rang. "Hey, Lin. Can you come play nine holes with me?" my dad asked. Apparently, he sensed that I had something on my mind.

"Sure, Daddy," I said. *Thank you, Lord,* I whispered under my breath.

I've never been a decent golfer. I'm convinced that every course I play has to call in a special repair crew for all the divots I create. That day was no exception. My head was not in the game. I had more important things on my mind—my dad's eternal soul. I mustered my courage with each bad shot. When we arrived at the ninth hole, I pulled out my putter and poured out my heart.

"Daddy, I need to talk to you."

"What is it, doll?" he asked as he smacked his ball into the hole without even looking up. It always amazed me how skilled my dad was at anything he tried.

I took a deep breath, opened my mouth, and out spilled a flood of emotion. "Daddy, I've been cheated. I haven't had you around all these years, and I've really missed out. I want to make sure that I get to have you around forever." My words were punctuated with sobs. The urgency of my message had overtaken me.

"Slow down, honey," Daddy pleaded. "I can barely understand you."

I breathed a prayer for peace, and the words continued to flow. "Uncle Hugh gave his life to Christ just a few weeks before he died. I'll get to see him again, and I want you to be there too."

"I know, doll," my dad said with conviction "and I'm going to do something about that."

"You do? You are?" I asked, not believing this independent man would be such an easy sell.

"Yes," my dad responded to both questions.

Immediately, I thought, *Well, let's do something right now.* But instantly I felt a check from the Lord. Now when the Lord tells me to talk, I'm good to go. But when he tells me to hush, that's a challenge. Still, I chose to listen to him in that moment. We finished our golf game, I hugged my dad goodbye, and he headed back to work while I set off for the pastor's office.

The pastor's wife was at the receptionist's desk. Phyllis was a sweet, soft-spoken lady with a heart full of compassion. I told her about my uncle's funeral and about the conversation that had just taken place on the golf course. "My daddy's so ready," I told her. "I just know that if Pastor Gales would talk to him, he would give his heart to the Lord."

"Don't you worry, honey, I'll tell the pastor everything you said." And she did.

Three weeks after the semester began, my sister and I received a letter from home. My step-mom was good at keeping us updated on the latest family news. "Your little sister is taking scuba diving lessons. The Mr. Lincoln roses are blooming beautifully. And by the way, the pastor came to visit and your dad and I gave our hearts to Christ." She said it so matter-of-factly that we read it over several times before it sunk in. When it finally did, we were yelling the good news to perfect strangers all over campus. "My folks accepted Christ!" There couldn't have been a better place to get news like this than on a college campus with a bunch of enthusiastic Christian students. People we didn't know were hugging us and crying. In an instant, God answered the prayer of a lifetime and I finally had the Christian family I had always wanted.

God was working all along; I just couldn't see it when I was moving through it. But now his plan is clear as I view what happened through the rearview mirror.

"That's so cool," Donnetta said, reaching for a tissue and handing me one too. "I've been so busy being angry at God that I haven't spent enough time looking in the rearview mirror. I've just climbed up a miff tree and told God to talk to the hand."

"Been there, done that, and it didn't work too well for me," I responded as we chuckled at her frank expression.

"Tell me about it."

"The only thing we can do is trust him and keep our eyes glued to the rearview mirror. H. William Webb-Peploe said, 'Don't try to hold God's hand; let him hold yours. Let him do the holding and you do the trusting.'"

"Well, nothing else has worked," Donnetta shrugged.

"In the Old Testament, when God did something memorable or miraculous for the children of Israel, he instructed them to erect a monument to commemorate the event. I think it's a faith-building tool to keep a record of those amazing times in our lives when we see God's hand of help and hope. We may not be able to see how God is going to provide a plan while we're in the middle of trouble, but hindsight shows he was handling things all along. Romans 8:28 says, "That's why we can be so sure that every detail in our lives of love for God is worked into something good" (MSG).

"I have a special journal where I write down all that God has done for me. When I add to the list, I spend some time reviewing previous blessings on my list and my trust is strengthened all over again. The Lord wanted his people to erect a monument so that they wouldn't forget his goodness and provision. I journal my Monumental Moments for the same reason. Donnetta, I want you to sit down with your journal, a pen, and a pot of your favorite tea."

"A pot?"

"Yes. This is going to take you a while. Look back over the landscape of your life and recognize God's care as you peer into the rearview mirror."

Truster Reconstructor

Reflect back on your life and journal those **Monumental Moments** when you can now see God's hand at work weaving a tapestry for good in your life. In particular, journal those experiences that didn't seem to have a good outlook when you were going through them but that turned out to be amazing blessings in the long run.

chapter 8

Pardon: The Healing Power of Forgiveness

D onnetta rushed in red-faced and panting. As she pushed open the door to accommodate Charlie, who was bundled like an Artic explorer, a gust of cool air blew in with her. "I'm sorry I'm late," she said as she unwrapped layers of clothes from her cherub-cheeked boy. Charlie peacefully played with the fringe on her hat as she wrestled off his baby bomber jacket.

"God has given you such a compliant child," I said as she gave him a set of toy car keys to play with. Charlie grabbed the keys and began making car sounds.

"He's smart too. Listen," Donnetta said. "He's mimicking the sound of a car engine. He's figured out the connection between keys and the vehicles they start."

"He is intelligent. Just like his mother," I commented.

"Interesting you would say that. I was late because I was checking online about available college programs. You keep saying that I'm smart, so I thought I would see what was available for me in the way of education."

"I think that's fabulous. You'll love school, and I think you'll do well. What do you want to study?"

"The dental assistant program is only two years long, and there is enough science that I think it would be interesting. I'm beginning to realize that for me to provide for Charlie, I need a career not just a job. Some programs provide day care and everything."

"That sounds like good judgment. I could see you being a very capable dental assistant. I'm glad you're pursuing your future," I affirmed.

"I know it will help provide for Charlie and me in the future, but honestly now, it will be great just to get away from my dad. Linda, I hope and pray that Charlie never feels about me the way I feel about my family."

"Actually, you're talking about the next layer of the emotional onion we need to peel."

"Yeah, and every time I peel a layer of the onion, I cry!" Donnetta quipped.

"Donnetta Jean, the more emotional bags you unpack now, the better you will be for yourself and your son." I motioned toward Charlie, who was crawling around on his blanket alternating between chewing on a toy Hummer and making racing noises. His crystal clear blue eyes framed in golden curls would melt any mother's heart.

"I'll do whatever it takes not to pass down the dysfunction of my family on to my precious boy," Donnetta said.

"I always appreciate your willingness to grow. God will reward you for that."

"He already is. Every day I feel closer to the Lord. I don't feel like he's Dirty Harry in the Sky anymore. I feel like he's watching out for me. It feels good."

"Donnetta, what if I told you there's a way to keep your dad from getting to you like he does—from eating your brain?"

"He does that, doesn't he? I guess I'm kind of obsessed."

"It's a paradox, but if you can find it in your heart to forgive him, it will loosen his grip on you."

Squirming in her seat, Donnetta protested, "When I was growing up in church, I heard so many sermons on forgiveness that I thought, *If one more preacher says, 'Just forgive and forget,' I'll scream.* How can I forgive when he keeps on offending?"

"I won't preach you a sermon," I said with a smile, trying to communicate that I was on her side, "but I believe that folks who say 'forgive and forget' haven't been required to forgive a lot. David's experience with King Saul in 1 Samuel teaches us to forgive and set boundaries.

But before we take a look at David, I'd like to share some things with you that I learned on my path to forgiveness. I think that may answer your questions."

"I know it sounds terrible, Linda, but I don't think my dad deserves to be forgiven," Donnetta said.

"I think you're ready to try. When you fired your dad, you let go of any expectations that he would be a supportive parent in the present, but nothing has been done about the hurt you sustained in the past. That's left you dragging around emotional baggage packed full of resentment. My old pastor used to say, 'Resentment does more to harm the vessel in which it's stored than the object on which it's poured.' You can dump that baggage and be free. Your renewed trust in Christ will empower you. He will walk through the process with you and give you the strength."

Donnetta was willing to listen. She was skeptical, but seeking.

In Ephesians 4:32, the apostle Paul encourages us, "Be kind and compassionate to one another, forgiving each other, just as in Christ God forgave you." That's a tall order. It can only happen with the Holy Spirit's power. But what if you're like Donnetta Jean and don't feel like your offender deserves to be forgiven? The Lord spoke to me about this very concern through a gentle-hearted lady named Iris, who shared with our small group at church. Iris opened up to our women about the sexual abuse she sustained at the hands of her biological father and declared, "Forgiveness doesn't make your offender right; it just makes you free." That profound statement started me on my journey to forgiving my mother. As a new Christian, I wanted to please God, but forgiving all of her abuse seemed like too much for God to ask. Just like Donnetta, I was skeptical but seeking, so I opened up the Bible to see what God had to say.

In Matthew, I read the words of Jesus, "For if you forgive others for their transgressions, your heavenly Father will also forgive you. But if you do not forgive others, then your Father will not forgive your transgressions" (6:14–15 NASB). How harsh, I thought, until I read what Richard

Foster had to say about this verse. In his book *Prayer: Finding the Heart's True Home,* Foster asks,

> Why is this? It is not that God begrudges his forgiveness, nor is it so hard to get God to forgive that we must demonstrate good faith by showing how well we can first forgive others. No, not at all. It is simply that by the very nature of the created order we must give in order to receive. I cannot, for instance, receive love if I do not give love. People may try to offer me love, but if resentment and vindictiveness fill my heart, their offers will roll off of me like water off a duck's back. If my fists are clenched and my arms folded tightly around myself, I cannot hold anything.
>
> But once I give love, I am a candidate for receiving love. Once I open my hands, I can receive. As Saint Augustine says, "God gives where he finds empty hands."[1]

In their book *Mood Swings,* authors Meier, Arterburn, and Minirth provide even further insight. "Choosing not to forgive allows others to continue to abuse us, as we endlessly relive their offenses."[2] That truth was brought home to me by a TV show, *The New Candid Camera.* I was wandering through the living room when I saw him on the screen, a large man with tufts of dark hair, a belly-roll hanging over his belt in front. If he'd had a name printed on the back of his belt, it would have been "Bubba." At that moment, I felt the Lord throw down a red flag on the field of my mind and whisper, "Pay attention, Linda. You're going to learn something here."

The host described the setup. A sign was posted on the cash register in a convenience store declaring, "We don't make change." A camera was

---

1. Richard J. Foster, *Prayer: Finding the Heart's True Home* (San Francisco: HarperSanFrancisco, 1992), 186–87.

2. Paul Meier, Stephen Arterburn, and Frank Minirth, *Mood Swings: Understand and Achieve a More Balanced and Fulfilled Life* (Nashville: Thomas Nelson, 1999), 207. Originally published under the title *Mastering Your Moods.*

hidden to record the responses of the people who were hassled by their gag. First, a middle-aged woman walked in and laid a few items down on the counter. The show host, posing as a cashier, rang up thirteen dollars and some change. The lady gave him a twenty-dollar bill and the mock store clerk put it in the register and closed the drawer. Rather annoyed, the woman informed him, "I believe you owe me change."

"Hey, lady, read the sign," the cashier replied. "We don't make change." At that point, the censors had to beep out the irate lady's protests.

Then Bubba shuffled in. He laid down his purchases. The total came to five dollars and some change. He too presented a twenty-dollar bill. The host-cum-clerk placed the twenty in the register and closed the drawer. Bubba uttered, "Uh, I think you owe me some money."

"Read the sign, buddy. We don't make change."

Bubba then turned on his heels and started to walk out of the store. The cashier moved from behind the counter and went after him. He tapped Bubba on the shoulder and inquired, "Hey, we owe you money, a decent amount of money. Why are you just walking away?" I'll never forget Bubba's response. Hands in his pocket fumbling for his keys, Bubba declared, "I decided a long time ago, I don't rent space in my head to nobody."

In that moment, I realized that I rented far too much space in my head to way too many people for far too few results! The authors of *Mastering Your Moods* were right. I was continuing the abuse as I ruminated about the resentment over and over again. I learned in recovery that "resentment is me drinking poison and hoping you die." When I stopped drinking from the toxic well of bitterness and self-pity, I had room in my life for healing and peace. What I learned about forgiveness, I was able to pass on to Donnetta.

Like me, Donnetta Jean had to stop renting space in her head to resentment. Choosing to let go of her bitterness didn't legitimize her father's behavior. He would still have to stand before God for his actions. It just removed her from the position of judge and left that job to Jesus, who was far better qualified. When she wasn't obsessing about her father's offences, she could crawl into his shoes and better understand what made him the way he was. His father had been a cruel, bigoted, abusive drunk who often beat him. Donnetta's dad never learned how to love from his father, so he couldn't pass that on to his daughter. By forgiving, Donnetta was choosing to stop the cycle of abuse from continuing to infect her son and even his children. It left space in her head to consider all of God's goodness and provision.

Donnetta was convinced that forgiving would be hard enough; she didn't know if she could forget. What a relief it was for her to find out that she wasn't required to forget. The Bible reveals this in the life of David, who was called a man after God's own heart. As the scene opens in 1 Samuel 24, David is on the run from King Saul. Some six hundred men have joined him, outcasts from society, and they are hiding in the caves of En Gedi. In the past, Saul had been like a father to David, but now because of petty jealousy, he is trying to kill David.

Saul, hot on David's trial, goes into a cave to relieve himself. David's men inform him, "This is the day the LORD spoke of when he said to you, 'I will give your enemy into your hands for you to deal with as you wish'" (1 Sam 24:4). David creeps up behind Saul unnoticed and slices a piece off the hem of his garment. But then David feels conscience-stricken and realizes that he could not kill Saul, God's anointed king of Israel.

I can see it in my head now. Saul saunters out of the cave. David and his men file out after him. "Yo, Saul. Does this look familiar to you?" I hear David shouting. "I could have slit your throat. I was this close," he boasts, holding up the piece of cloth. "But I didn't think that would be pleasing to the Lord." Then David begins an impassioned speech in which he refers to Saul as his "father." You can imagine the confusion and frustration filling the fugitive's head: *As God is my witness, Saul, I don't know what your beef is with me. I killed a giant for you, fought valiantly beside you. I even played my harp to calm your frazzled soul.*

Finally, David says,, "I have not wronged you, but you are hunting me down to take my life. May the LORD judge between you and me. And may the LORD avenge the wrongs you have done to me, but my hand will not touch you" (v. 11–12).

Saul responds, "You're right; I'm wrong. You're good; I'm bad."

David didn't say, "It's all good, Saul. Let's just forget about all your abuse. Go back to the palace. We'll and hunt and fish together. I'll play my harp for you and everything will be hunky-dory." David knew that Saul's heart hadn't changed. I believe that God himself imparted that wisdom to his servant David. Sure enough, two chapters later Saul is trying to kill David again.

The life-changing truth of this passage is so subtle it could slip past you if you aren't paying attention. The final sentence in 1 Samuel 24:22 reads, "Then Saul returned home, but David and his men went up to the stronghold."

David didn't slaughter his offender even when he had the opportunity and the encouragement from his troops. He didn't let hatred for Saul consume him, but neither did he rush back to the palace and set himself up to be disappointed again by his jealous father figure, Saul. I find it interesting that the New International Version uses the word *stronghold* to describe the crags of En Gedi. I believe those crags were as much of an emotional stronghold for David as they were a physical one.

We see that the Bible's guideline isn't "forgive and forget." It's "forgive and set boundaries." Setting boundaries requires that we maintain a healthy distance from our offenders and spend time with the Lord. He will either give us strength to speak up to bullies or thick skin to ignore them. Like David, we need to retreat to our stronghold, distance ourselves from the damage, and invest in the empowerment we get from seeking God.

The more Donnetta understood about her recovery, the more she realized she had to move. Instead of feeling trapped into staying in her parents' home, she determined to find a way out. Proximity to her father made it difficult for her to continue healing from his emotional abuse. She had already fired him from the dad role (see chapter 2). That freed her from expecting him to be there emotionally for her in the present; forgiving him freed her from carrying around the pain of the past. Now she determined daily to do life differently than either of her parents. Instead of being preoccupied with the pain, she would spend that time in prayer to break the cycle of abuse.

I shared with Donnetta that the person she needed to forgive the most was sitting in her seat. Out of reaction to her dad's abuse, she had made some very poor choices for herself. The entire time she acted out of despair and self-loathing, she told herself she knew better. But she did it anyway. That left her feeling stupid and shameful. Unless she dumped that baggage and forgave herself, that guilt would continue to keep her from being all she could be for the kingdom of God. Micah 6:8 instructs, "He has showed you, O man, what is good. And what does the LORD require of you? To act justly and to love mercy and to walk humbly with your God." The Lord wants us be merciful to ourselves.

Donnetta discovered that she needed to clear the air with God and forgive him too. He gets blamed for a lot of the things we bring on ourselves. If we find we're angry that life isn't going the way we planned, then we need to climb out of our miff tree and stop telling God to talk to the hand. We have to let him off the hook or we'll distance ourselves from the only one who can truly help us. When we make peace with him, we discover that our best interest is his first priority.

Of all the things that I learned about forgiveness, I most wanted Donnetta Jean to understand the significance of recognizing God's restoration. That was illustrated for me one afternoon as I sat in my living room listening to a lady who was new to our church share her story. Sarah Ann's life of abuse and neglect made my life sound like a picnic in comparison. As we cried and prayed together, she looked up from her Kleenex and made a remark that jolted me awake. Sarah Ann said, "I'm so glad you've had pain in your life, Linda, because I know that you can understand what I've been through. I've never been able to share any of this with another Christian before, much less a pastor's wife. But I can tell you all of this crazy stuff because I knew you'd get it."

After she left, for the first time in my life, I got on my knees and thanked God for my pain. I thanked him for the empathy I had for Sarah Ann and so many others because I did get it. And the blessing of helping people access the abundant life God has for them, fills my tank to overflowing. I wouldn't trade my pain for easy street because of all it has taught me. I knew that someday Donnetta would feel the same way, but first we had to jettison some unwanted baggage.

"Donnetta, if you want to continue to grow in your Christian walk, then I have an assignment to help you in this forgiveness process."

"After hearing about Bubba, I don't know what to expect," she said with a nervous grin.

"We're going to do some more writing, but this time it will be in letter form."

"Who am I writing?" Donnetta asked.

" Your dad." Donnetta rolled her eyes and stiffened.

"Your dad will never see the letter, so you can be as honest as you need to be."

"How will it benefit him if he never sees it?" she asked.

"The letter is to benefit you. You're going to bring it back here, and with the Lord's guidance, we'll process what you've written to help you forgive your father and let go of the attendant baggage."

"Just like that? It seems too easy."

"That's because you haven't written the letter," I said. " Before you write it, I want you to earnestly ask God to reveal every bit of resentment that you have tucked away in the nooks and crannies of your heart. Then grab a pen, paper, and a cup of coffee. Take a couple of hours with no interruptions to pour out your pain onto the page. Are you left or right-handed?"

"Right-handed. Why?"

"Then I want you to start writing your letter with your left hand," I said. "The experts say that it helps to access the right side of the brain, where feelings are centered. I have found it also helps people get in touch with the vulnerability they felt in their early years. As you write about situations that happened as you grew older, you can switch and use your right hand. Your letter to your dad needs to be as thorough as you can possibly make it."

"I'll do my best," Donnetta sighed.

"I know you will, and I can't wait to see what the Lord will do with your willing heart."

Truster Reconstructor

Now it's your turn to dump the baggage of bitterness that has rented space in your head for too long. Like Donnetta Jean, write a copious and thorough letter to your offender. Don't hold back. Get out all of your resentment and frustration. The next chapter will show you what to do with what you've written.

chapter 9

Provision: Jettisoning Emotional Baggage

"M y mom has Charlie today because I just got back from register-ing for school," Donnetta announced, her eyes dancing as she settled onto my sofa.

"Congratulations! I'm so proud of you," I beamed.

"That's not all," she continued, barely able to contain her excite-ment. After I left here last week, I went home and called the college. The woman on the phone said a new class starts in three weeks and this would be the last day I could register. I needed to have $150 by today. Linda, I have an extra $150 in my account that my ex-husband's aunt gave me for my birthday. Can you believe it?"

"Actually, I can. God has your back."

"It's hard for me to doubt that when things like this happen."

"Girl, I believe he's got a lot more blessings where that came from. Remember our goal when we started was to take your dad's face off of God. That gets easier as you see the Lord taking care of you, doesn't it?"

"Yeah. I couldn't have planned this any better. It's too perfect to be a coincidence. This has got to be God thing," Donnetta answered.

"I couldn't agree more. I believe there's another God thing available for you today. We're going to clean out the clutter that keeps you from fully connecting with him. Did you finish the letter to dad that we talked about at the end of our last session?"

"I did," she reported, heaving a sigh. "You were right. When I wrote with my left hand, I felt so vulnerable. I was that fragile little girl again—feeling alone and unloved. It was hard. I'm glad I had registering for school to keep me preoccupied so I wouldn't have to rent space in my head to all this junk until I could get here and do something with it."

"Then let's get busy. Will you read it to me, please?" I asked.

"I have to read it?"

"Your reaction to the information as you read it is the catalyst for the work that will take place here today."

"I've already cried so much writing it. What if I don't have enough emotion left to process all of this?"

"We'll let the Lord worry about that. He seems to be working things out pretty well for you these days, don't you think?"

"I can't argue with you, Linda. It's hard to read the part I wrote with my left hand, but here it goes."

Dear Dad,

I always wanted to call you Daddy, but you never were one. I remember wanting so badly to have you pull me up in your lap and make me feel special. I don't ever recollect that happening. On my fifth birthday when mom took me to get my picture taken, I felt so beautiful dressed up in pink ruffles with my hair full of ringlets and bows. Then we stopped by the garage on our way out and Mom said, "Doesn't Donnetta Jean look beautiful, Don?"

You had a look of such contempt on your face when you laughed at me saying, "Pretty for a bunny rabbit. If she would stop sucking her thumb like a big baby, then she would look like a buck-toothed rabbit."

I was crushed. I haven't felt pretty since that day. You taught me that I couldn't trust myself. I thought I was a beauty; you made me feel like a bother. I knew then that I would never measure up to your expectations, but that didn't stop me from trying.

When I was ten, I won the spelling award for the entire grade. But you didn't come to school for my award ceremony. I heard you tell mom that it wouldn't matter how I spelled because I was just going to stay home and take care of some man and his kids. I never told you about any of the awards I got in school after that.

When Andy started messing with me, I wanted to tell you, but I was scared. I figured you would yell at me and make it my fault. It made me feel so sick inside. I would stand in the shower for hours trying to feel clean again. I wanted so badly to have someone to protect me from him. That someone should have been you, Dad.

Tears were stinging Donnetta's eyes as she read that last line. It was hard not to rescue her, but I knew that feeling the hurt was the necessary first step in peeling away the layers of pain. "This is where I switched to my right hand," she informed me. I handed her a tissue and nodded for her to keep going.

I grew to hate you for lining us up in the living room and giving the whole family your self-righteous speeches on how we're all going to hell because nobody has any manners anymore or how God hates lazy people. My guts would churn because I knew I had homework to do, but I had to "be respectful" and stay and listen until you unwound since you were the head of the household. You made sure we never forgot that.

When I asked mom for sanitary pads, you made fun of me for starting my period. You told me it was a woman's curse for being stupid enough to fall for Satan's lies, eat the apple, and then use her womanly wiles to deceive the male. I felt excited about the changes in my body and glad to be feminine until you got involved. How could you manage to ruin every good thing, Dad?

Then there was the day Misty died. That cat crawled into my lap to comfort me so many times, and now she was a mangled mess in the middle of the road. I could barely get my breath. I was so devastated I thought I would fly apart. You were so cold and uncaring. You had no sympathy for me or that innocent creature that never hurt you or anybody else. When you informed me that God let Misty die to punish me, I gave up on you and God, then and there.

I made a bunch of bad choices while I was running from God. Most of them were to tick you off, Dad. I didn't think you deserved a good kid. You would have bragged that I was good because of you, but the truth is that anything good I ever accomplished was in spite of you. So I did dumb things and ended up feeling like used goods. Then I gave myself away and ended up with Eric, who confirmed my worthlessness to me.

Living with you, Dad, is a nightmare. I'm so afraid that you will rub off on Charlie, and I want him to be nothing like you. I'm scared to try anything new for fear that I will fail and prove you right—that I am flawed and not worth loving. I'm afraid of becoming involved with a man again because Eric was so much like you, and twice is two times too many. I'm tired of feeling stuck, and I pray that the Lord can get me unstuck. Maybe he will do the same for you, Dad.

I'm done.
Donnetta

Wiping her eyes, she handed me the letter. "When I said 'thorough' you took me seriously, didn't you?" I remarked, wanting to validate the hard work she had done to get in touch with her feelings.

"Donnetta, Jesus asked a crippled man at the pool of Bethesda if he wanted to be healed. That seems like a strange question to ask someone who had been crippled since birth. I think Jesus knew that if the man had wanted it badly enough in all those years, he could have found a way to make it happen. So he asked, 'Are you ready to let go of what is crippling you?' That's the same question that I'm asking you today. It's so easy to wrap ourselves up in our pain and let it define us. Then we become victims, not victors. That changes when we welcome his healing power. Are you ready to be healed?"

"Linda, I'm sick and tired of being sick and tired, so I guess that means yes. But I've been carrying around this pain forever. I don't know what we can do to make it go away."

"We're going to dump our baggage on Jesus. He knows what to do with it. First Peter 5:7 tells us to 'cast all your anxiety on him because he cares for you.' The King James Version uses the word *care* for *anxiety*. I heard a preacher say that the nets fishermen used in Jesus' day weighed two hundred pounds. So when I'm casting my care on the Lord, I'm not flicking my wrist and watching the line soar out over the water. I'm heaving a heavy burden of hurt at his feet. Few people would know as well as Peter how hard it is to dump our disappointment at the feet of Jesus. We can only imagine the hurt and shame Peter had to endure after he betrayed the Lord he loved. And it was Peter, the fisherman, who wrote this. If it worked for Peter and made him into the powerful preacher we see in the book of Acts, it will work for you, girlfriend. Let's take this to the Lord in prayer, shall we?"

I asked Donnetta to get as comfortable as possible. I invited her to adjust the pillows behind her back and handed her some tissues in case she began to cry. "I don't want you to have to interrupt the flow of the Holy Spirit to wipe your tears," I explained.

"Oh, great! So you expect me to blubber like a baby."

"I expect God to peel away the layers of your pain," I said, "and sometimes that's just like an onion—we peel a layer and we cry."

When Donnetta was settled, I said, "I'm going to start our prayer, then I'll let you know how to respond when it's time." With that I bowed my head, and so did Donnetta Jean.

"Lord, I thank you for bringing Donnetta here, and I praise you for your transforming power," I began. "We come to you right now asking you to heal the pain from the past that is hindering the present. You said, Father, that we would know the truth and the truth would set us free. You also said that you would send us the Holy Spirit and that he would lead us into that truth.

"So we invite your Holy Spirit's presence into this room right now. Donnetta, I want you to feel the Holy Spirit as he moves down through your forehead. Feel his warmth move in and feel the tension in your temples drain down your cheeks. As the stress drains down, feel your eyes relax and roll back in your head. Feel your jaw hang loosely on its hinges. Feel your chin drop to your chest as you let all the stress in your face roll down your cheeks and drip off the end of your chin.

"Now feel the warmth of his presence move down through the back of your head, your neck, and your shoulders. Feel all of the tension in your neck and shoulders drain down your arms and drip off the end of your elbows. Feel the breath of his presence fill your lungs. Breathe out any tension and pressure you feel. Let the rest of the tension in your arms roll down your forearms and drip off the end of your fingertips, like warm candle wax moving down your arms, pulling your tension and stress with it.

"Now feel the Holy Spirit as he moves down through your throat, your chest, and your gut. Feel him press the stress out of your chest as his presence moves in. Feel any tightness there draining down into the sofa. Feel the air move into your lungs. Feel the air move out of your lungs.

"Now feel him move down through your thighs, and down through your shins. Feel the tension pressed out of your legs as the Spirit's warmth moves in. Feel any residual stress roll out the end of your toes.

"Now I want you to see your mind like a giant computer screen in front of you. It's cluttered with faces and images. One by one, I want you to project those faces and images onto large, billowy clouds that are hanging right around your head. I want you to see Charlie's smiling face; he's laughing as he chews on his stuffed skunk. Now I want you to project him onto a soft, puffy cloud and watch as he giggles with delight and drifts heavenward.

"See your mom there on the computer screen of your mind. She works so hard. Project her off the screen of your mind onto a cloud and watch how she sails out of sight. Each time you project a face or an image, you notice that the computer screen in front of you becomes more and more blank.

"Take your right hand and move dad off the screen of your mind. Set him onto a comfortable cloud and let him go. See him drift upward.

"Take your left hand and move your worries about your finances and your future onto a nearby cloud and release them. I want you to continue to project any faces or images onto the nearby clouds until the computer screen of your mind is completely blank.

"Now watch as that blank computer screen grows larger and larger in front of you until you are surrounded by a huge expanse of white. There in the white I want you to picture Jesus. It could be a picture you've seen in a child's Bible or a Sunday school classroom or just the picture you see in your mind's eye as you pray. When you can see him there, I want you to describe him to me. What's he doing? What color is his hair? What color are his eyes? Remember, you can't fail with detail. Describe to me the Jesus you see in your mind's eye."

Donnetta slowly said, "He's wearing a white robe that's tied around the waist. He has long brown hair. His eyes are brown. They're loving and compassionate. His arms are outstretched." Tears formed in her eyes.

"Who is he reaching out to?" I asked.

"He's reaching out to me," her voice cracked.

"He wants to hug you with one of those no-strings-attached hugs. Will you let him?"

Still praying, she nodded her head and wiped her tears.

"Feel his strong arms around you. Feel the sleeves of his garment wrap around you like a warm quilt. Rest your head on his broad chest and relax. In Matthew, Jesus tells us, 'Come to me, all of you who are weary and burdened, and I will give you rest' (11:28). Let his strong arms completely support your weight as you let go and relax. Feel the fabric of his garment beneath your cheek. Hear his heart beating as you rest on his chest. How do you feel, Donnetta?" I asked softly.

"Safe."

"Rest in that safety," I instructed. After a moment's pause, I continued. "Both Jesus and you notice that he can't seem to reach his arms completely around you because you're wearing a huge backpack. It's filled with the emotional baggage that's kept you from embracing his fullness for a long time. He would love to help you dump this baggage, but he won't do it without your permission. Can he help you get rid of it?"

"I need him to," she responded with conviction.

"I want you to notice that the backpack is lighter as Jesus pushes up on the bottom. Hook your thumbs under the straps and swing it down between him and you. As you flip open the top flap, you see a large rock inside. The rock is huge. No telling how long it's been in there. Its surface has jagged edges that would lacerate your fingers if you tried to lift it. Scrawled across the top of the rock is the word *fear*. Jesus wants to dispose of the fear rock; but for your own healing, you need to wrap something around it. You need to wrap words around what you fear. You need to confess the damage it's done in your life and explain why you are ready to be rid of it. Can you do that?" I questioned.

Clearing her throat, Donnetta didn't miss a beat. "Lord, I am so tired of being afraid of everything. I'm afraid of going to school; I'm afraid of not going to school. I'm afraid Charlie's father will try to take him. I'm afraid I'll be stuck living with my parents forever and I'll grow to become as miserable as they are. I'm afraid I'll go back to the way I was—distant from you, Lord, and making dumb choices because of it. This fear is crippling me. I ask you to take it from me. Will you get rid of the fear rock?"

"Donnetta, watch as Jesus reaches into the backpack and grabs the fear rock . The sharp edges don't even cut him because he's God. Watch him pitch it so far that you lose sight of it.

"Now you notice another rock that was tucked underneath the fear rock. It is just as jagged and just as heavy. Written across the top of this rock is the word *hurt*. You've been caring around the hurt for way too long. The Lord will get rid of that rock if you let him. But as with the fear rock, you need to articulate the hurt and give God permission to unpack it."

Donnetta took a deep breath and started, "This pain is destroying me. It's makes me negative, and I hate being that kind of person. It's a darkness, and I need get rid of it so that I can feel a lightness in my load. I don't want to be defined by all of the bad stuff that's happened to me anymore. I don't want to keep tripping over the hurts in my life. I want to leave them all right here and move on.

"And Lord, I especially need to let go of the pain of feeling like I'm not good enough for my dad, that I'm flawed and don't measure up." She spoke those words with a heavy sigh.

"Can Jesus take the hurt rock?" I asked.

"Absolutely!"

"Donnetta, I want you to watch Jesus reach into the backpack and snatch the hurt rock. He flashes you a smile as he tosses it away easily, like it's a pebble.

"Tucked under the hurt rock is another one, just weighty. Scrawled across the top of that rock is the word *resentment*." As I talked, Donnetta Jean nodded in affirmation.

"The Lord wants to rid you of your resentment, but first you need to confess your part and give God permission to take it away. Can you do that?"

"Lord, I am so ready to be free of this poison in my life. I don't want to keep holding on to all of this bitterness toward my dad. Resenting him doesn't make him any better, and it's making me a lot worse. Jesus, you've been showing me lately how rough he had it as a kid. No wonder he was such a messed-up father for me and my brothers. I need to forgive my brother Andy too. In many ways, Dad was toxic to him too, and he has to live with himself now.

"While we're at it, Lord," Donnetta was a on a roll, "I need to lay down my hostile thoughts for Eric. I don't want to end up resenting my son because I can't stand his father. I have to confess, Lord, I have felt that way at times, and I want those feelings gone. I give you permission to take all of the resentment from me."

"This time," I explained, "Jesus needs you to participate in getting rid of the resentment rock. It's not because he can't do it alone; it's because you need to be part of the process of ridding yourself of the resentment.

So I want you to see yourself clutching one end of the large rock as Jesus holds the other. It doesn't cut you because Jesus is protecting you. Feel his strength empowering you as the two of you send the stone soaring."

The Lord was doing a mighty work, so we continued to unpack Donnetta's bags.

"As you look down, you see another brutal boulder that had been hidden by the resentment rock," I said quietly. "Etched on the surface of this rock is the word *anger*. Your anger has been fueled by your resentment. Once again, if you want to be free of your anger, you need to confess it. Express the harm it's done in your life. Ask God to eradicate your rage."

"Lord Jesus," Donnetta earnestly prayed, "I've been angry with my dad for being insensitive to my needs and my mother's needs too. I'm angry with him for his judgmental remarks. And for his hypocrisy—acting like he's Mr. Holy at church and being a royal jerk at home. Most of all, I'm angry because he never made me feel like he loved me.

"God, I confess I have been angry with you for letting all the bad stuff happen in my life. I now realize that many of the negative circumstances were a result of choices I made to get back at my dad. Please forgive me for that." Tears of remorse flowed freely down Donnetta's cheeks. It was cleansing.

"Can he have the anger rock?" I asked, helping her to finish the job she had started.

Donnetta Jean nodded and dried more tears.

"I want you to watch as Jesus reaches into the backpack, grabs the anger rock, and hurls it 'as far as the east is from the west' (Ps 103:12). He remembers it no more, like the Scripture tells us.

"Underneath all of the other rocks, you find a very formidable rock labeled *self-loathing*. It's been at the bottom of your backpack for a long time. In order for you to move ahead, it's got to go. You know what to do," I said.

"Lord, Linda is right. I have hated myself for as long as I can remember. I've always felt like I deserved the bad treatment I got because I was worthless. I'm sick of feeling flawed. I don't want to keep sabotaging anything good because I don't feel like I deserve it." Exhaling in relief, Donnetta asked, "Will you please take this rock?"

"Notice the strength in the Lord's arm as he stoops to pick up the rock of self-loathing," I said. "Watch as his large hand wraps around it and launches it effortlessly out of sight. See him wink at you as he does; he's so proud of you for letting go.

"Now, Donnetta Jean, I want you to notice that Jesus is holding out a rock of his own, a perfectly symmetrical, polished stone that is radiating heat and light. You realize that it's for you. As you take it with your hands, you're amazed to discover that it weighs practically nothing. As you hold it, you feel the light and the warmth of the Holy Spirit strengthening you. Where you felt fear, you now feel peace because you know that God is in charge and is watching over you. In the place of hurt, you now feel rejuvenated by the Lord's restoration. Instead of resentment, you feel a flood of forgiveness for yourself and others. Reconciliation fills your heart, replacing the anger. Having let go of the self-loathing, you're free to feel the unconditional love of God as his Spirit infuses you with his power. Soak up the warmth of the Spirit," I instructed.

"The Lord wants to give you a sentence or two that will resonate as truth in your head for the rest of your life. What's he saying to you, Donnetta?"

With a tearful smile, she responded, "Jesus says he will always love me. He paid a dear price with his own life to prove it."

"That will resonate in your mind forever to affirm how crazy God is about you," I assured her as we finished our healing prayer.

"Donnetta, we need to leave this place for now, but you can come back here any time you need to rest in your loving Savior's arms. Before we leave, is there anything you would like to say to Jesus?"

"Yes. Thank you, Lord, for the love I feel. Please, don't ever let me go."

As Donnetta rested calmly in the Lord's presence, I concluded our prayer. "Dear Father, I want to thank you for caring enough to custom-design the healing that each of your children needs. I ask that you, who began a good work, continue that work in Donnetta Jean. Inspire her to come into your presence often for the support her soul craves. We praise you for your powerful provision for us. In your Son's name we pray. Amen."

As she opened her eyes, I asked Donnetta, "How do you feel?"

"Weary but wonderful." she proclaimed.

"You will be tired. You've just undergone spiritual surgery. Like a physical procedure, it takes a lot out of you. Just after dumping my emotional baggage, I found that the Lord continued to provide insights into my behavior and future. I believe he was always ready to share them, but I was so loaded down with baggage that I couldn't receive the good things he had to offer me. Be prepared in the next few weeks for fresh revelations from your Lord and Savior. And get some rest."

"Gladly," Donnetta responded. "I feel like I've just lost a hundred pounds. "

"At least. I'm not giving you any other assignment this week. I think you've done enough today."

"I'll say! See you next time," Donnetta replied, practically floating out of my office.

Truster Reconstructor

Take time to walk through the **Trust-Building Prayer Exercise** to unpack your emotional baggage with God's help.

chapter 10

Priorities: Making the Main Thing the Main Thing

Toddling into my office in a pint-size yellow rain coat, complete with hat and galoshes, Charlie seemed to be enjoying the rain far more than his mother, who was struggling to keep up with him. "He was so excited to wear his new rain slicker today," she announced.

"Who could blame him? He looks like such a big boy today."

"He is a big boy," Donnetta responded. "He's started attending day care two mornings a week while I go to class. Grandma watches him the other two days. Doesn't she?" Donnetta cooed as she turned her attention to her dimpled-cheeked boy. "Can you say *Grandma*?"

Charlie responded, "Ga'ma."

"You're smart like your mama." Charlie grinned from ear to ear. "How exciting! What do the two of you think about your new adventure?"

"Charlie is thrilled to have other kids to play with, and the day-care provider is great with him. I love being in school. I had to write an essay for college entrance, and the registrar praised my writing. I didn't tell her that I get lots of practice because my counselor makes me write all the time."

"Who knew that would be a side benefit?" I quipped. "I'm proud of you; you're a college student!"

"It's more work than I thought. I'm finding it's harder to fit everything into my day. I love studying, and I could do it all night, but I don't want to neglect my son. I have to be at school so early that I miss my prayer time. Just my luck that when I finally realize how much I value my time with the Lord, my schedule gets too busy for it." She shrugged. "I'm not feeling the closeness that I had with God, and I don't like that feeling.

"I want to be a good mother, and I know that God has been helping me do that. Right now there is so much that pulls me off focus. My schedule is only part of it. The other distraction is—or as you say it, Linda, 'Honey, let me tell ya'—there are some really cute guys on campus. I've been asked out three times since I've been there."

"What do you expect? You're bright, blond, and beautiful," I affirmed.

"I would have argued with you about that a few months ago, but I feel a lot differently about myself these days."

"Confidence is attractive. Guys want to be around women who are comfortable in their own skin—and these days, you are."

"I went to a study group and pizza with one of the guys, Tim. I agreed to go because I wanted to connect with more students in my class. At least that's what I told myself. The truth is Tim is gorgeous, and it would be real easy to think about him 24/7. But he's twenty-eight, still lives at home, and has never had a steady job.

"The study group met at a coffee shop next to a pizza parlor. After studying, a few of us went next door. Tim was charming, and it felt good to be pursued again. I managed to resist because I realized this is the same behavior I fell into with Eric, and his best friend before him. At that time in my life, I had to be in a relationship to feel worthwhile, even if I knew the person wasn't good for me. Now that I am finding my worth in God and myself, I don't want to go back to that old way of thinking."

"Donnetta Jean, that's music to this counselor's ears."

"Don't get me wrong," Donnetta continued, "I want a husband and a father for Charlie. I just don't want to throw myself at some fella's feet because he tells me I have nice eyes. I really want to do what God wants, but when I get the attention that I crave, it's hard not to cave."

"Donnetta, the Lord knows you want a husband and a family, and he wants to give you what your heart desires. It says so in Psalm 37:4. So far in your healing process, you have let go of your pain, offered up forgiveness, and seen God's undeniable provision. Now it's time to establish your priorities. You keep God in the number one spot when you wait patiently on the Lord, intentionally focus on his will, and never forget his power to provide. Then you will WIN. Let's delve deeper."

"An acronym. Do I get a story today too?"

"You know my spiritual gift is making a short story long," I teased as she settled in for some teaching time.

How about you? Are you ready to WIN? Here's your formula, starting with the first step: Wait on the Lord. The psalmist said, "I waited patiently for the Lord; he turned to me and he heard my cry. He lifted me out of the slimy pit, out of the mud and the mire; he set my feet on a rock and gave me a firm place to stand. He put a new song in my mouth, a hymn of praise to our God" (Ps 40:1–3). This scripture tells us to wait on God for strength and answers and he will lift us out of our mess and plant us in a position of strength. But the answers and the strength don't come without the wait.

When I was the director of our church's high school youth group, I wanted to share with them the significance of spending time in God's presence, of waiting on him. In conversations with young people, I heard things like, "I met this guy and he had on a cross like my grandpa's cross, so I thought this must be a God deal." Or, "She loves Mustangs like I do, so this must be God and stuff." (From my vantage point, I thought it was more like hormones and stuff.) I wanted them to slow down enough to hear from God, so I directed the group to Psalm 46:10, "Be still, and know that I am God." That's when I discovered that the talk I was preparing for these young people was actually for me.

In the Hebrew, several words are used for *still*. When David says, "He leadeth me beside the still waters," in Psalm 23 (KJV), the word for *still* means "comfortable" or "quiet." There is also a word for *still* as in, "Are we still listening to Madonna?" Neither of those words is used here. The word for *still* in Psalm 46:10 is *raphah*, which means "to cease, to be idle, to let go, to draw toward evening"—like you're sitting on your front porch swing with no agenda but to sip sweet tea and wait for the lightning bugs to show up. The root word for *raphah* is *rapha*, which means "to mend by stitching, to make or cause to heal or repair." This scripture informs us that we have to hush up, calm down, and be quiet so God can thoroughly make us whole.

I tend to be a person with a lot of plates spinning in the air all the time. Being still doesn't come naturally to me. Yet it never ceases to amaze me how the Lord fills my spiritual tank when I surrender my agenda and wait patiently at his feet. Making God number one in those quiet moments puts my priorities in line and brings peace to my tattered soul.

The *I* in WIN is intentionally focus on God's will. We have to choose every minute to make God the main thing in our lives. That point is powerfully portrayed in the story of Daniel. He was taken from Israel to a foreign nation and trained for three years for the king's service. During training, he was offered the best food and wine from the king's table. But Daniel believed the Babylonian diet was not in keeping with his Jewish ideals. He wanted fruits and vegetables, not the king's rich menu. So Scripture says, "But Daniel purposed in his heart that he would not defile himself with the portion of the king's delicacies, nor with the wine which he drank: therefore he requested of the prince of the eunuchs that he might not defile himself" (Daniel 1:8 KJV).

The line "purposed in his heart" makes clear Daniel's intentionality. It would have been easy to partake of the foreign fare that was constantly in his face, but Daniel was determined to make God his number one priority. He obeyed the Lord and waited patiently for him to act. After a ten-day trial, he looked healthier and better than any of the young men who ate the king's rich food (v. 15). Daniel proved that his new diet brought blessings in return.

The *N* in WIN warns us to never forget God's power to provide. Solomon instructs us in Proverbs 3:5–6 to "trust in the LORD with all your heart and lean not on your own understanding; in all your ways acknowledge him, and he will make your paths straight." Those words helped me focus on God to get me through the dark days in my mother's house. In our doubt, it would be easy to languish in despondency over what we perceive is God's inaction or jump ahead of his timing and do things for ourselves. The latter didn't work too well for Sarah, Abraham's wife, as we can see illustrated in Genesis 16.

Sarai, as she was called at the time, learned the hard way to wait for God's provision. Running out of patience with God to give her a son, she took things into her own hands. She sent her maidservant Hagar to sleep with her husband. There's not a woman in any culture who couldn't see what was coming! Hagar got pregnant and lorded it over Sarai. Not a smart move. Abram, in true phlegmatic fashion, stayed out of the fray and let the girls fight it out. Sarai saw the opportunity to get even and mistreated her maidservant (v. 6). Hagar ran away, but God found her and took care of her—even a lowly maidservant. (I love that part!) And the son Hagar bore has been causing trouble ever since.[1] It never pays to step ahead of God. He will provide in his perfect time. We can't forget that.

It would have been easy for Donnetta to run ahead of God. She felt lonely and vulnerable, and there were men pursuing her. But God was working out his best for her like he promised in Psalm 37:4, "Delight yourself in the LORD and he will give you the desires of your heart." Her job now was to trust him. As she learned to WIN, she could focus on making the main thing the main thing in her life.

I learned a powerful lesson about putting God first during the time my husband and I call God's Divine Squeeze. It was after our third child, Ashley Rose, was born. With five-year-old Sarah and three-year-old Jake, I had survived croup, colic, and ear infections. My pregnancies had been uneventful, making me the perfect candidate to have the local midwife deliver my third baby. I thought I had motherhood down. But nothing could have prepared me for what lay ahead.

When Ashley was eleven days old, I took her to our family pediatrician for a checkup. Dr. Frisbee was an older man with a jovial manner and a quick wit. But today he wasn't joking. His ominous grunts and groans sent fear up my spine. When he called down the hallway for an

---

1. Traditionally, the Arabs are considered descendants of Ishmael, Hagar's son. If so, that would make Sarai's choice the origin of the continuing conflict between the Arabs and the Jews.

associate to come and "listen to this" as he held a stethoscope to my helpless baby's chest, I felt my knees grow weak.

"What's wrong with my baby, Dr. Frisbee?" my voice cracked.

"Linda, I would just feel more comfortable if she could be seen at the university."

"The university is five hours from here," came my troubled response.

"Yes, and I'd like you to leave right now. Can you call your husband to pick you up here?"

What a wise man. He knew that if I'd had any idea of what was really happening, I would have imploded. Instead, I called my husband Bruce, tried to explain what was happening without falling apart, and asked him to arrange care for the two older kids. Then I raced home to pack.

In less than an hour, Ashley, Bruce, and I were heading north. As we pulled out of the driveway of our four-thousand-square-foot ranch on six acres overlooking the Applegate River, I tried not to think about what was ahead of us. My thoughts turned toward a conversation I'd had with Bruce on a summer evening less than a year before as we sat on the deck.

We hadn't always lived in such extravagance. With four degrees between us, Bruce and I graduated from a Christian college ready to save the world for Christ. Right away, we were hired to do youth ministry at a church with a handful of kids. Within a few months, more than a hundred kids were showing up every Monday night. Young people were coming to Christ and lives were changing. We were thrilled and thought other leaders in the church would feel the same way. But some of the leaders were upset because many of the kids didn't come on Sunday morning. And when I heard one of the power brokers of the church stand up in a board meeting and say, "These kids who come on Monday night don't pay tithe," I tucked my idealistic tail between my legs and walked out of church that night.

My husband decided that we would take a year out of ministry, a little breather. We got into sales, and I'm here to tell you, my husband could sell spots to leopards! We now had two preschoolers, so I worked from home making phone calls and keeping records while Bruce held sales meetings and did follow-up. We made beautiful money together!

One year out of ministry turned into eight, and before long we had more money than we knew what to do with. Our accountant insisted that we invest in real estate, so Bruce decided to buy his dream home in Oregon.

On an evening in late summer only a few months after we moved in, we sat on the deck admiring the view. Bruce turned to me and said, "Sure is beautiful, isn't it?"

"Sure is," I agreed.

"Sure did work hard to get here, didn't we?" came his second question.

"Sure did."

Then just as I was thinking it, Bruce said, "Sure is empty, isn't it?"

"Sure is," came my sober reply. Neither of us knew what to do with those feelings, so we quickly changed the subject. And now here I was driving away from the home I thought I could never live without, and suddenly it meant so little to me. I just wanted my baby to be all right.

When we arrived at the university hospital at nine o'clock that night, a team of cardiologists was waiting for us. They whisked Ashley away for tests. After what seemed like an eternity, they brought back my weary, hungry baby. Then a tall dark-haired female doctor stepped forward. "Ashley has several life-threatening heart defects. She will need many heart surgeries in her life to correct them," the kind doctor informed us, pacing herself and pausing periodically for my sobs to subside. "Her first will be tomorrow morning. We have an emergency surgery scheduled for her at ten o'clock."

Psalm 34:18 in *The Message* reads, " If your heart is broken, you'll find God right there; if you're kicked in the gut, he'll help you catch your breath." I literally felt the Lord holding me up, helping me breathe.

Ashley miraculously made it through that surgery, and as I drove my fragile child home wondering what the future held, not knowing how I was going to hold my family together, I remember saying to God, *The things that mattered so much to me—my cherished house, my valued antiques, the RVs in the driveway, all mean so little to me now. I just want to keep my baby.*

Because her heart was so weak, Ashley's immune system was compromised. So she spent most of her early years in the hospital. At one point, we knew the names of all the nurses who worked on the pediatric floor. Bruce had been on the road for the past year doing sales and promotion, but now he found he couldn't muster the gumption to leave again. "I'm afraid I'll get a call while I'm in Timbuktu telling me that she's gone. I couldn't live with that," he'd say. I knew how he felt. I didn't want to be away from my blue-eyed bundle either.

So we had to generate income by selling things. First went the antiques—those precious pieces that I spent hours procuring. At one time they meant so much to me, but now all I thought was, *Take them, Lord. Take the 1850s hand-painted Waterbury clock. Take the walnut dresser and the Persian rug. Just let me keep my baby.*

Then it was the motor home. The Jeep CJ was next. I didn't care. *I don't care about losing these things, Lord. I just don't want to lose my Ashley,* I prayed.

Finally, it was the house. My home was my pride and joy. I lost count of the hours I spent pouring over designer magazines, selecting just the right wallpaper and color schemes, fretting over what my friends would think about my décor. When the house sold, I didn't care. With the real estate market depressed, we didn't get a dime out of the sale. But at least we got out from under the payment, and I still had my baby girl.

One morning as I was gathering up the courage to tackle packing up the house, Bruce posed a question: "Honey, since we're obviously going to be poor, do you want to be poor for God again?"

If he had asked me that one year earlier, I'm ashamed to say, I would have laughed in his face. But in the few months after Ashley's birth, I'd spent a lot of time on my knees and I was hearing from the Lord again. "Why not?" I replied. "At least if we're in ministry, we'll have purpose in the midst of our poverty."

So my husband and I packed up our little family and moved six hundred miles away to a church that paid us $500 a month and a house that rented for $450. And every month God miraculously provided for us through the loving people in our church family.

My husband was the music minister, and we taught a large young-adult Sunday school class. We hadn't been there long when a couple in the class threw a party for the whole group. One of the dear ladies who worked in the nursery at church insisted on taking care of our kids so we could attend. In her fourteen months of life, Ashley had either been with her dad or me around the clock, so it was hard to say yes. But I was so hungry for conversation that did not include medicine or breathing treatments, I consented.

It was a wonderful evening of fun and fellowship—until 8:30. We got a call from the babysitter: "I don't know what happened. Ashley was playing just fine, and then she crawled up in my lap and went limp. I felt her head and she's burning up."

I had seen Ashley spike high temperatures before, so I knew she had to be seen by the doctor immdiately. Bruce and I left the party, picked up Ashley, and rushed to the children's hospital. The emergency room doctor suspected infection, so he prescribed medication. Because she had to take so many antibiotics in her short life, she had developed allergies to many of them. So the doctor wanted us to stay at the hospital for a few hours in case Ashley's throat swelled shut.

It was already late on Saturday night. "Honey, there's no need for both of us to lose sleep all night," I told my husband. "You have to lead worship tomorrow, so why don't you pick up the older kids and head home. I'll stay with Ashley." Knowing Sarah and Jake were worried and needed to see him, he conceded.

When my husband left, I told the attending nurse I was going to step outside for a minute. She nodded as I walked outside of the waiting room into the night air with my lethargic baby in my arms. In the loudest voice I could muster in my mind so as not to wake her, I screamed under my breath, "OK, Satan, you take your best shot. You have taken everything—the cars, the toys, the house, and now you want to take her. You hear me, and you hear me good, if you take her, you need to know, I will not turn my back on God. Do you hear me? I'm in this for the long haul, and even if she's gone, I will not turn my back on God!"

At that very moment, my precious Ashley, who had been as limp as a dishrag for the past three hours, woke up in my arms saying, "Hungry, Mommy." We left the hospital that night, and in the days and weeks that followed, I watched Ashley gain weight and grow stronger.

I didn't realize until that hot, sticky night in the hospital parking lot that when we delight ourselves in the Lord, he becomes our heart's desire. That experience was a defining moment in my Christian walk. As my old pastor used to say, I did "bid-ness" with God. I believe there comes a time when every believer has to decide to fish or cut bait, or rather to become fishers of men or be content to bask in the boat.

That time came for Donnetta Jean right there in the office that afternoon. She purposed in her heart to put God first. We prayed together and asked for the Holy Spirit's empowerment to keep the main thing, the main thing.

What about you? Are you ready to WIN like Donnetta Jean? Review the scriptures mentioned above and add these. *Wait on the Lord:* "Yet those who wait for the LORD will gain new strength; they will mount up with wings like eagles, they will run and not get tired, they will walk and not become weary" (Isa 40:31 NASB). *Intentionally focus on God's will*: "Steep your life in God-reality, God-initiative, God-provisions. Don't worry about missing out. You'll find all your everyday human concerns will be met" (Matt 6:33 MSG). *Never forget the Lord's power to provide:* "My grace is sufficient for you, for my power is made perfect in weakness" (2 Cor 12:9).

Truster Reconstructor

List your top three priorities in your journal. Invest in each one every day. To keep yourself accountable, keep a record of what you do.

chapter 11
Passion: Warts and All

I see you've been to McDonalds," I said, observing that Charlie clutched the latest free toy from his Happy Meal.

"Isn't he fetching with ketchup in his hair?" Donnetta remarked.

"He's discovered french fries and free toys. Your life will never be the same."

"You're telling me. He yells, 'Stop!' from the back seat every time we pass a play yard with Ronald McDonald."

I inquired, "Now that you've been in school for a while, is your schedule getting any easier?"

"It's difficult, no doubt. I'm limiting my study-group time so that guys with broad shoulders and big blue eyes don't distract me," Donnetta confessed. "That's helped me maintain my priorities, and I'm finding ways to make the most of my time by listening to teaching tapes on the way to school. It's not quite as tank-filling as my prayer time in the early morning, but it keeps me focused. Last week, I listened to your CD series on that verse in Zephaniah."

"He Delights in You; Rest in His Love?"

"That's the one. I didn't know that verse existed. But that's not saying much. I didn't even know there was a book called Zephaniah in the Bible, and that's such a cool verse. I put it on the cover of my daily planner so I could memorize it: "The LORD your God is with you, he is mighty to save. He will take great delight in you," she paused, seeming lost.

"He will quiet you with his love, he will rejoice over you with sing-ing," I finished for her.

"I can't forget the singing. That's practically the best part," she said.

"I'm proud of you, Donnetta. Most adults tell me their brain is too old to memorize, and they are not much older than you. Zephaniah 3:17 is a verse worth committing to memory. I think it's so significant, I devoted an entire retreat to it."

"I wish my Sunday school teachers had shared scriptures like this one when I was younger. All I ever heard about was the things we should do: 'You should remember your quiet time with God, or he won't bless you. You should read your Bible everyday, or you don't love God enough. You ought to pray and not fall asleep. God hates sinners, so you shouldn't be angry and cross.'"

"You know what they say in twelve-step recovery?" I interrupted. "Don't 'should' on yourself and don't 'should' on anyone else."

"I won't forget that one," Donnetta laughed. "My dad had so many rigid rules, and when he used the Bible to support his selfishness, it was too much for me. I ran from him and from God. But now I'm realizing that God loves me not because of what I do, but just because of who he is."

"Donnetta, it's been my prayer since we began this process that you would come to know how much God loves you, warts and all. He is passionate about the person sitting in your seat." Tears welled up in her eyes as I shared what I knew to be true about God's heart.

"It's taken me a while to get my head around this," she confessed. "I don't want to forget and become apathetic toward God again."

"You're already ahead of the game," I affirmed. "I was thirty-five years old before I realized that I could be a human being instead of a human doing. God used a difficult situation in my life to prove that to me.

"The message of the Lord's unquenchable love was reinforced for me when I read about the life of Elijah. His story demonstrates some valuable steps for staying connected to God so we can feel his passionate care, no matter what we're going through. And it proves to me that the

Lord loves all of his children, warts and all. Now I want to share with you what I learned."

In 1 Kings 16:30, the Bible declares, "Ahab son of Omri did more evil in the eyes of the LORD than any of those before him." How would you like to have a rap like that? Before we blame Ahab, we need to take a look at his father's contribution. Omri fostered an alliance with Phoenicia, and to solidify that pact, he gave his son to be married to the daughter of the Phoenician king. Enter Jezebel! Her name is still iconic with horrid women everywhere.

When Jezebel married and moved into Ahab's home, she brought with her 450 prophets of Baal and 400 prophets of Asherah. It's important to note that Ahab was the king of Israel, God's chosen people. Jezebel wasn't polluting the home of a foreign king with all these false gods; she was parading them into the palace of the king of God's children!

The Lord looked for a faithful prophet to present a warning to King Ahab. Despite their pursuit of other gods, the Lord was still passionate about his people. So he sent Elijah the Tishbite to confront the wayward king. The prophet decreed, "As the LORD, the God of Israel, lives, whom I serve, there will be neither dew nor rain in the next few years except at my word" (1 Kings 17:1). I can hear it now: "Hey, Ahab. You know how Baal is supposed to be the god of the weather? Well that's bogus, buddy, because there is only one true God, and I'm going to prove it to you."

It took guts for Elijah to go before Ahab; Jezebel was already persecuting the prophets of God. Many of them went into hiding, but Elijah remained faithful. Now we see how passionate God is about his servant. The Lord sent his prophet to the one place in that drought-ridden land that would dry up last, the Kerith Ravine. Then God sent ravens that "brought him bread and meat in the morning and bread and meat in the evening, and he drank from the brook" (v. 6).

Ravens were considered unclean birds by the Jews, so Elijah could have questioned God about his judgment in this matter. "What are you doing here, Lord? Haven't I been taught since I was a good little boy growing up in the synagogue not to contaminate myself with what's unclean? And now you want me to eat food from the beak of an unclean bird?" Here's where we learn from Elijah a valuable requirement for staying connected to God: we must *trust* him. That's simple but not easy. It didn't make sense to his Jewish sensibilities. But God told Elijah to eat the bread provided by the ravens, and Elijah did because he trusted the Lord.

Have you ever been there? Perhaps you've found yourself wondering, *Why did I have to lose my job, God? You know I tithe on my earnings.* Only later does God give you a job with better pay and more time to spend with your family. You've asked, *Why did I have to be the one diagnosed with this autoimmune deficiency?* But eventually you realize that your illness brings the family closer to each other and closer to the Lord. Or you've asked, *Why did this tree fall on my house, God? With all that's on my plate, and now this.* Weeks later, you reflect on how the tree collapsing your garage got you talking to your neighbors. Then you invited them to church and they received Christ, so now you'll be neighbors eternally in heaven. Despite your situation, even if it doesn't make sense, we learn from Elijah that we will feel God's passionate care when we trust him.

Then the brook dried up and God told Elijah, "Go at once to Zarephath of Sidon and stay there. I have commanded a widow in that place to supply you with food" (v. 9). Do you recall where Jezebel was from? She was from Sidon—in Phoenicia. Of all the places the Lord could have sent his servant, he sent Elijah to the birthplace of his worst enemy! If I were Elijah, I would have wondered why God couldn't send me to the home of some nice little Jewish mother who would feed me kosher food, tweak my cheek, and tell me what a good boy I was. But Elijah trusted God, so he went to Zaraphath.

There he encountered a widow who was gathering up sticks. He asked her for a drink and some bread. "'As surely as the Lord your God lives,' she replied, 'I don't have any bread—only a handful of flour in a jar and a little oil in a jug. I am gathering a few sticks to take home and make a meal for myself and my son, that we may eat it—and die,'" (v. 12). Notice that the widow didn't say, "As surely as the Lord lives." She said, "As surely as the Lord *your* God lives." This poor widow knew a true believer when she saw one. There had been plenty of hungry people traveling through her town with drought in the land, but she sensed something different about this one. She knew Elijah was a man of God.

Elijah told the woman not to fear. He promised that if she took care of him, God would take care of her throughout the drought. And he did. "The jar of flour was not used up and the jug of oil did not run dry, in keeping with the word of the LORD spoken by Elijah" (v. 16). It never ceases to amaze me what God can do in the lives of those who obey him.

Some time later the widow's son became ill and died. "She said to Elijah, 'What do you have against me, man of God? Did you come to remind me of my sin and kill my son?'" (v. 18).

Then Elijah took the widow's son and carried him to the upper room where he was living. He prayed: "O LORD my God, have you brought tragedy also upon this widow I am staying with, by causing her son to die?" (v. 20). Elijah's prayer reveals our next step to feeling God's passionate care: We *tell* him how we feel. He already knows anyway. But when we get hurt or frustrated with God because things aren't working out the way we think they should, we distance ourselves from him. We tell him to talk to the hand when what we need to do is to tell him all about it.

As Elijah prayed for the boy, his life returned to him, and he lived. The prophet brought the boy to his mother saying, "Look, your son is alive!" (v. 22).

She responded, "Now I know that you are a man of God and that the word of the LORD from your mouth is truth" (v. 24). "At first," the woman claimed, "I knew that you were a believer, but now that I have seen God work in my life in an up-close and personal way, I am a believer too! I recognize that the God you speak about is the one true God."

Why did the Lord allow hardship to come into this woman's life? Why did this widow's only son die? So that she could have a soul-saving encounter with the living God. Today, that lady is walking streets of gold. I don't think she's minded her hard times, do you?

Then God told Elijah it was time to confront Ahab again. Assembling the prophets of Baal and the people of Israel, he questioned, "How long will you waver between two opinions? If the LORD is God, follow him; but if Baal is God, follow him" (18:21). Then he called for a show-down on Mount Carmel. "Get two bulls for us. Let them [the prophets of Baal] choose one for themselves, and let them cut it into pieces and put it on the wood but not set fire to it. I will prepare the other bull and put it on the wood but not set fire to it. Then you call on the name of your god, and I will call on the name of the LORD. The god who answers by fire—he is God" (vv. 23–24). And the people said, "Bring it!"

Elijah let the prophets of Baal go first. They placed their bull on the altar and prayed from morning until noon. Then Elijah began to taunt them. "'Shout louder!' he said. 'Surely he is a god! Perhaps he is deep in thought, or busy, or traveling. Maybe he is sleeping and must be awakened'" (v. 27). The *Living Bible* says, "Perhaps he is talking to someone, or is out sitting on the toilet." (It really says that!)

So the prophets of Baal shouted louder and began to cut themselves as was their custom. They prayed until evening, "but there was no response, no one answered, no one paid attention" (v. 29). Isn't that just like Satan to lure you in just to let you down?

Then Elijah said, "Move over, boys, you're about to see God work." He built an altar with twelve stones to represent the twelve tribes of Israel. Then he dug a trench around it and instructed his helpers to fill four large water jars and drench the bull on the altar—not once, but three times! He wanted to make sure that those watching knew this was no trick: if this soaking wet sacrifice caught fire, it would have to be a miracle.

"At the time of sacrifice, the prophet Elijah stepped forward and prayed: 'O LORD, God of Abraham, Isaac and Israel, let it be known today that you are God in Israel and that I am your servant and have done all these things at your command. Answer me, O LORD, answer me, so these people will know that you, O LORD, are God, and that you are turning their hearts back again.'" (vv. 36–37). It's amazing to me what can happen for the kingdom of God when we don't care who gets the credit. Elijah gave glory to God.

He could have said, "Well, I am a pretty brave guy. I did confront Ahab—not once, but twice. And there was that miracle with the widow's son. Did you hear about that? Folks, resurrection is a very new concept!

Let's face it. I've got it going on." How many times have we seen people in the Christian community elevate their giftedness rather than the giver of that gift, the Spirit of the living God? Not Elijah. He let the people of Israel know the source of his power.

"Then the fire of the LORD fell and burned up the sacrifice, the wood, the stones and the soil, and also licked up the water in the trench" (v. 38). It's enough to make you shout, "Hallelujah!" "When all the people saw this, they fell prostrate and cried, 'The LORD—he is God! The LORD—he is God!'" Then Elijah commanded them to seize the prophets of Baal. "Don't let any get away!" he ordered. Then he had the false prophets taken down to the Kishon Valley and slaughtered.

When I first read this, I thought, *How harsh!* But then I realized that this drastic move to clean up Israel was an example for us to clean up our own lives. When we find sin in our hearts, we have to cut it out and make no apology for it. That's the next step in staying connected to God despite the circumstances. If we want to feel God's passionate care, we have to trust him, tell him how we're feeling, and then *tighten* our grip, even when it's tough to do—especially when it's tough to do.

If we're going to stay connected to the Lord, we can't dip our toes in the tide pool of sin. We can't say, "I can sleep with my boyfriend. Other girls in the church do." Or, "I can drink with my friends after work. I don't get drunk, just a little tipsy." We can't indulge in church gossip and excuse it with, "I just wanted you to know so you could pray." If we want to feel God's passion for us, we can't waver between two opinions like the children of Israel. We have to tighten our grip and embrace a lifestyle that honors the Lord.

Then Elijah informed King Ahab that rain was coming. The prophet sent his servant to the seashore to check for rain clouds, but nothing was there. He did it again seven times, and only on the seventh visit did the servant see "a cloud as small as a man's hand rising from the sea" (v. 44). There had been no rain for years—three years according to some commentaries. If I were Elijah, I would have wanted the Creator of the universe to come up with something a little bigger than a man's hand to prove my prediction of rain to end the drought. But Elijah was faithful in spite of the circumstances.

He sent his servant to tell Ahab to hitch up his chariot and head toward the sea before the rain stopped him. Then the power of the Lord came upon Elijah and he gathered up his garments and outran Ahab's chariot for fifteen miles! Another marvel!

When Jezebel found out what Elijah had done to her precious prophets of Baal, she sent him a vindictive message stating that she was going to do to him what he had done to her prophets. In other words, he was dead meat! "Elijah was afraid and ran for his life" (19:3). He ventured a day's journey into the desert, plopped down under a broom tree, and prayed that he might die. Here was a man who had experienced the miraculous provision of the ravens, raised the widow's son from the dead, called down fire from heaven, and outran a chariot for fifteen miles. But now he is hiding under a tree afraid of one ungodly woman!

My heart resonates with his story. I fear that if there were a broom tree in my backyard, that's where I would park my carcass. Even though I can look at the landscape of my life and the amazing miracles God has performed on my behalf, I still find myself, at times, crouching in fear and circling the drain. Despite all the times God has come through for me, I have a black belt in whining. I forget his benefits too easily despite the admonition of his Word to forget them *not* (Ps 103:2).

As Elijah lay there, he fell asleep. "And all at once an angel touched him and said, 'Get up and eat'" (1 Kings 19:5). Sometimes when we find ourselves overwhelmed with discouragement, what we need is a nap and a snack because fatigue makes cowards of us all. Elijah "looked around, and there by his head was a cake of bread baked over hot coals, and a jar of water" (v. 6). So he ate and drank and took another nap.

"The angel of the LORD came back a second time" (v. 7). Some Bible commentators believe that, in this instance, the angel of the Lord is the preincarnate Jesus Christ. If so, in Elijah's time of doubt and fear, the Lord Jesus himself showed up to give him what he needed. He offered his hopeless helper food for strength, drink for refreshment, support, and help despite Elijah's attitude.

God could have thundered great disapproval from the heavens at his faithless follower. "How dare you, Elijah? After all the miracles I have performed for you. Who do you think you are, you ungrateful whiner?

Where is that smite button?" But this scripture confirms that this is not God's style. He loves us in spite of our faults, thank goodness! You need to know that when you're under that broom tree, quaking in your boots with faithless fear, Jesus will show up for you too. He's passionate about the person sitting in your seat.

Elijah ate the food that was provided and was strengthened for the journey ahead. "He traveled forty days and forty nights until he reached Mount Horeb, the mountain of God. There he went into a cave and spent the night. And the word of the LORD came to him: 'What are you doing here, Elijah?'" (v. 9). No condemnation, no shame, just a concerned, "Whassup?"

Then Elijah launched into a tattletale story about how bad he had it. He ended his tirade by saying he was the only prophet of God left and now the people were trying to kill him too. Have you ever been there—thinking you are the only one going through this tough time, that no one else can understand your pain? In reality, there were seven thousand people who had not bowed a knee to Baal. The Lord was exercising immense patience with his self-pitying servant. Elijah's heavenly Father had a powerful lesson for him.

"The Lord said, 'Go out and stand on the mountain in the presence of the LORD, for the LORD is about to pass by.' Then a great and powerful wind tore the mountains apart and shattered the rocks before the LORD, but the LORD was not in the wind. After the wind there was an earthquake, but the LORD was not in the earthquake. After the earthquake came a fire, but the LORD was not in the fire. And after the fire came a gentle whisper" (vv. 11–12).

Every day the whirlwind of our daily schedule batters and beats us. We face the shake, rattle, and roll in the earthquake of everyday life. We find that our time is consumed with putting out fires as the immediate crowds out the eternal in our lives. But the scripture is clear that the Lord was not in the whirlwind or the earthquake or the fire. This passage illustrates the next step to feeling God's passionate presence in our lives: we have to *take time* to hear God's gentle whisper. If Elijah wanted to hear the healing balm of God's truth, he had to idle down long enough to hear the "still small voice" (v. 12 KJV).

In that quiet moment, the Lord revealed his plans to the prophet, how he had already provided for his replacement and what would happen to others around him. But just as we learned in the last chapter, we have to be still enough to receive the restoration that God has for us.

Have you ever been there, that point when the whirlwind, the earthquake, and the fires have consumed you, and life is requiring more out of your truster than you can muster? You find yourself underneath a broom tree, discouraged, depressed, and quaking in your boots. I have. It was when Ashley Rose was five years old and facing her third heart surgery. She had just started kindergarten. The first two surgeries had stretched us all, and neither my precious daughter nor I were ready for another one.

As her heart grew weaker and weaker, it became harder and harder for me to trust the Lord. One dismal winter night, the surgeon's office called. They had a bed and a surgery date for Ashley. After lengthy instructions about her extended stay at the hospital, the surgeon soberly added, "Given the difficulty of a surgery of this magnitude and her fragile state, I need you to prepare yourself not to take her home."

It took a moment for me to catch my breath as his words sunk in. All I could say was, "Doctor, I deal with a lot of people in many stressful situations, but I need to tell you, I don't know how to do that myself."

Every day, I had to drag myself out from underneath the broom tree and put one foot in front of the other. The Lord was all I had, so I simply had to trust him. But I had to tell him how I was feeling. I couldn't keep it bottled up inside of me; I felt like a ticking time bomb.

My schedule was always packed, either doing something with the church or my children. I had no idea when I could find time to process all that was swimming around in my head. So one day in early spring at the church's first picnic of the season, I asked another mother to watch my two older kids, left Ashley with her dad, and took a long walk. I found myself in a cove. I plopped down on the beach and finally stopped stuffing in all of my feelings. "You are God!" I shouted in the empty cove. "You could bat an eyelash and heal this child." It felt good to get it out, but my words seemed only to echo in the pine trees that afternoon.

The day came when we had to drive our precious little girl to the hospital at UCLA. We had barely settled in when the nurses whisked her away, leaving me with a sinking helpless feeling. For nine long hours I waited under that broom tree fearing that the other shoe was going to fall. So I tightened my grip on life, recollecting every scripture, sermon, and song that had ever brought me hope. At ten o'clock in the evening, my husband and I were finally allowed into cardiac recovery.

Weighing only thirty pounds, Ashley looked so tiny and weak lying there with a machine breathing for her. There was an IV, electrode pad, or a drainage tube on every square inch of her frail little frame—except for one spot on her head where a precious nurse from Los Angeles was rubbing Ashley's hair into a part and speaking comfort to her as she fitfully slept.

"Wow," the nurse informed us, "this is amazing. Your daughter's like getting better by the minute. This is like a miracle and stuff!"

"Honey, this is a miracle!" I informed her.

Every few minutes, someone came over to remove another tube or wire. As she continued to improve, the nurse sent us out briefly so they could remove her ventilator. I went back to her bedside as soon as they would let me. By now the whir, the whiz, and the white noise of all the machines had died down. Ashley was sleeping peacefully. Her awesome nurse, who hadn't left her side, said she was going to sit down at the nurse's station across the room and have a Pepsi. I told her to drink a case of Pepsi; she had earned it.

As I stood at the foot of my daughter's bed watching her chest rise and fall, thanking God for her every breath, I noticed the sun coming up. Just over my shoulder the gentle morning light was bleeding through the blinds. In the quiet of that moment, I could hear the gentle whisper. *The other shoe didn't fall, did it, Linda? It's always fallen. At least that's how you feel, isn't it? But I'm here to teach you that I'm going to take care of you. Daddy's got you now. It's going to be all right.*

Ashley continued to recover, but there was no guarantee that she wouldn't have to go through this again many more times. However, I was guaranteed that God would get me through no matter what life dealt me.

After I told this story at a women's retreat, a precious pastor's wife, Marie, came up to me and shared how she didn't get to keep her Ashley. Just after her daughter's sixteenth birthday, she was in a fatal car accident. "Linda, it was like you said about Elijah. I had to trust, as hard as it was. I had to throw myself out of bed every day and make myself go through the church doors and be around people. Because what I really wanted to do was stay home, crawl into bed, and turn my electric blanket on high—forever.

"I had to tell God how I felt pretty regularly for the first three months. I felt angry. I was sacrificing to serve him, and it didn't seem fair. Since I was taking care of his children, I felt he needed to take care of mine. Having it out with God didn't distance me from him. In those moments of honest sharing, I learned more about myself and God than I would have otherwise.

"Holding on to everything I had learned about the faith, I tightened my grip. The verse that got me through was Deuteronomy 33:27, 'The eternal God is your refuge, and underneath are the everlasting arms.' Every time I read it, I heard the Lord's gentle whisper. It's been two years, and I'm still hearing it. It gets me out of bed every day and helps me fall asleep at night."

Marie felt the Lord's presence in a palpable way when she needed him most. "I realized that God loves me in spite of myself," she declared. God longs to be there for you too. Feel his passionate care. No matter what your situation, God's got your back.

Truster Reconstructor

Practice the **Steps to Connection** with God: *trust* him, *tell* him how you're feeling, *tighten* your grip, and *take time* to listen to what the Lord has to say. Write down what you learn about the nature of God with each step.

What has the Lord done for you lately? Journal it. Now, what do you plan to do for him? Dream big!

chapter 12

Purpose: The Real Thing

Charlie charged into my office brandishing a stuffed elephant. He ran over and jumped into my lap to show me his new toy as Donnetta Jean opened a bag full of toy cars and pop-up books. She looked like the quintessential college student with a heavy backpack and a harried look on her face.

"What do we have here?" I asked.

Charlie called out, "El-fant, el-fant."

"He's talking so well," I remarked.

"I know. He practically learns a new word a day." Turning to her enthusiastic son, Donnetta said, "Tell Linda where we are going today after we leave here."

"Da zoo!" he replied, kicking with his diminutive Adidas.

"The zoo! How fun is that? You're a blessed boy," I responded, giving him a squeeze.

Charlie squirmed down from my lap and headed toward the corner where he knew I kept a few toys.

"I hope he's a blessed boy," Donnetta commented as she patted the blanket on the floor motioning for Charlie to sit down by the pop-up book full of jungle animals she had laid out.

"I just came from a lab," she sighed. "My plate is so full now. I don't want to neglect him."

"You're making time to take him to the zoo. That's hardly neglect-ful," I corrected.

"This is the first nice day we've had, and it's my only free afternoon for the next six weeks," Donnetta lamented.

"Yeah, and you're spending it with your son," I reminded her. "I'm delighted you get to spend some quality time together."

"I just wish I had more of it. School is hectic, but I'm trying not to get neurotic. I was constantly fretting in high school. I always felt such pressure to perform. I know now I had a deep need to prove myself to my dad so I felt like I had to be perfect. That made me crazy in school. Sometimes before tests, I would be awake all night.

"I can't afford that now. I have a child to take care of. It forces me to lean on God. I try to use the Daily Dialogue and talk to the Lord all day long, but my classes are so demanding, and I feel compelled to make all A's. The hard part is that I know I can do it if I obsess, but then everything else suffers. I don't want Charlie be shortchanged."

"Perfectionism is a pernicious problem," I said, "especially when we feel compelled to prove ourselves to someone who can't be pleased. Because my mom was like your dad and nothing I ever did was good enough, I wasted a lot of time fretting about my performance and trying to measure up. Then I discovered a couple of valuable nuggets of truth from Scripture that set me free. The first one was in the story of Mary and Martha.

"Whenever Jesus came to Bethany, he knew he had a place to stay and a meal at the home of Mary, Martha, and their brother Lazarus. On one of those visits, he was teaching while Mary was sitting at his feet listening to what he had to say. 'But Martha was distracted by all the preparations that had to be made. She came to him and asked, "Lord, don't you care that my sister has left me to do the work by myself? Tell her to help me!"' (Luke 10:40). Martha was one of those bossy, perfectionistic types. We can tell because she was one of the few people who had guts enough to give orders to the Son of God!" Donnetta chuckled as I continued my story.

"The Lord responded, 'Martha, Martha…you are worried and upset about many things, but only one thing is needed. Mary has chosen what is better, and it will not be taken away from her' (vv. 41–42). No doubt Martha felt a deep need to impress the master, but it caused her to be consumed by the immediate and miss the eternal."

"I'm a lot like Martha. I can get going on a plan and find it hard to surrender my agenda," Donnetta observed.

"Me too. That's why I value this story so much. You will really relate to what the Lord showed me.

"In verse 41, the words *worried* and *upset* are used in the New International Version. In the King James Version, those words are *careful* (or *care-filled*) and *troubled*. The word *troubled* is also used in the King James in John 5:4–7 to describe how the angels stirred the water at the pool of Bethesda. God healed whoever got in the water when that was happening. It would be easy to think that when we see the word *troubled* in Luke 10 that it means the same thing as it does in John. But further study reveals that two different words are used for *trouble* or *troubled* in the Greek.

"In John 5, the Greek word for *troubled* is *tarazo*. It means 'stirred up' or 'upset' like we see with the waters described in this chapter. But in Luke 10, the word used for *troubled* is *toorbadzo*. It means 'to make trouble.'"

"There's a big difference," Donnetta nodded her head.

"I thought so too. It helped me realize that, like Martha, I make a lot of trouble for myself fretting about things that either don't matter or that God has already take care of. All the while I could be resting at the feet of Jesus like Mary.

"A missionary friend of mine was fond of saying that if Jesus had told Mary to get in the kitchen and help Martha, they both could have sat down at his feet sooner. My friend was a driver like me. The Lord knows our nature, and he knows that in order to feel like she was good enough, Martha would have found more to do. So the Lord was saying to her, 'Martha, Martha—honey, sugar, darlin'—you are making way too much trouble for yourself. Serve store-bought food and sit a spell at my feet. Who cares if the placemats aren't pressed or the plates don't match the peas? You don't have to be the Martha Stewart of Bethany. Martha, honey, it's you I want—not your performance.'"

"Jesus has a Southern accent now?" Donnetta Jean laughed nervously.

"I knew you wouldn't let that one pass by!

"Donnetta, don't make the same mistake I did. I've spent enough time for the both of us in wasted worry wondering if I measured up. I had to pull a 4.0 grade point average, be president of every club, struggle for first chair in band, etc. Whether it was my weight, grades, housekeeping, or parenting, I made myself neurotic trying to prove that I was worth something. One day in my late twenties, after chasing two preschoolers all day, cleaning up the same mess again and again, and wondering why I had agreed not only to host a Bible study group but to lead it, I collapsed in a heap of exhaustion. The words of Matthew 11:28 echoed in my head, 'Come to me, all you who are weary and burdened, and I will give you rest.'

"I had just yelled at my kids for being kids, and now they were cowering in their rooms. Feeling guilty, discouraged, and wondering why I felt so compelled to be Superwoman, I picked up my Bible to read the passage I had remembered: 'Come to me, all you who are weary and burdened, and I will give you rest. Take my yoke upon you and learn from me, for I am gentle and humble in heart, and you will find rest for your souls. For my yoke is easy and my burden is light' (vv. 28–30).

"At the time, I didn't know why I felt compelled to look up the word *rest* in Strong's Concordance—maybe because I needed to understand it so badly. I know now it was the Lord's leading. The word *rest* in this verse translates the Greek word meaning 'exempt.' I cried as I heard the Lord say, 'You're exempt from your striving, Linda. You're enough.'

"'Take my yoke upon you and learn from me for I am gentle and humble in heart.' I read the words again. When I'm in my hypervigilant overachiever mode, I am anything but gentle and humble. I'm harried, angry, and impatient. And everyone around me can attest to that."

"I know what you mean," Donnetta agreed. "When I let my plate get too full, Charlie pays the price." She pulled her groggy son into her lap along with his elephant pop-up book.

"That's why my poor children were cowering in their rooms that day, fearing that the mommy dragon was going to breath fire again," I added. "Reading those verses in Matthew instructed me to take Christ's yoke, learn from him, and I would find rest. In that moment I heard the Lord say, 'Trade ya, Linda. You take my load and I'll take yours.'"

"So an 'easy yoke' is not a joke," Donnetta Jean quipped as she laid her sleeping son on the sofa next to her.

"You're so quick. I think that's exactly what that verse says. Constantly trying to prove myself is anything but an easy load. That scripture reminds me that I am exempt from needing to be perfect in order to prove I'm lovable, and that Christ in me is my only hope of glory (Col 1:27)."

"It's so easy to fall into old patterns, " Donnetta remarked. "These days I am more able to ignore my dad's remarks. He reminds me all too often that I had to take the GED to finish high school. What he doesn't know is that all of my overachieving left me with burnout. I realized in counseling that all my efforts were an attempt to prove to him that I could do it. Ironic, isn't it?"

"You don't have to prove to anyone—including yourself—that you're good enough. Jesus took care of that at Calvary. Donnetta, there are people whose purpose in life is to prove themselves to a disparaging parent, living or dead, and they don't even know it. There's the stockbroker who creates a huge company and amasses great wealth, but he's never satisfied. Deep inside he's trying to compensate for his dad's continued disappointment that his son never played professional baseball. There's the anorexic college student who studies day and night trying to outrun the corrosive criticism of her controlling mother. The stories, sadly, are endless."

"It's easy to see how a person could get trapped and not even realize it," Donnetta commented.

"It creates such bitterness in people's lives when they waste their efforts trying to win the favor of someone who is incapable of giving it to them. I heard a speaker say that we can labor to get to the top of the ladder only to find that it's leaning against the wrong building."

"That's scary," Donnetta said, "but I see how it could be true."

"Not when we live each day with God's purposes in mind.. I see you invested in his plans for you, girl. You're doing an excellent job as a mom, and you're a great student of recovery. You've grown so much since we started this process. Don't let Satan tell you otherwise. You know he'll sell you a case of discouragement if you'll buy it! You're living your life proactively, not reactively, and you are pursing a purpose with a future and a hope."

"Thank you," Donnetta sincerely responded. "I feel like I've come a long way. I don't want to live my life to please my dad, but I don't want to just live it for myself either. I want to do something for God.

"I was thinking about my purpose last week, just before they announced a mission trip to Mexico at church. I felt like this was a real God thing. Then as I was walking out of church, my small-group leader introduced me to one of the trip coordinators, a friendly lady named Madeline. She asked me about school and told me how much they could use me to help the dentists that are going. I told her I didn't have any experience, but she kept assuring me that I had more training than most. Then I really thought it was a God thing. What do you think, Linda? Am I ready for something like this?"

"I think that sounds awesome!"

"The group is going the week of spring break, and Charlie will be with Eric's parents. They're good people. They feel the same way about their wayward son that I do. And they think the sun rises and sets in their grandchild, so I guess we feel the same way about Charlie too." Donnetta Jean flashed a smile that told me she was feeling more confident.

"I'll have a few months of dental assistant training under my belt. Hopefuly, I'll know something by then that could help the dentists. Madeline says my two hands will be plenty of help."

"I'm sure that's true. This is wonderful opportunity. I'm thrilled you want to do it!"

"I'm not nearly as worried about the dentistry part of the trip as I am about the testimony part," Donnetta said. "I know there will be questions about God and my faith, and I don't know what to say. Still, I feel like I need to give back to the Lord for all he has given me. A week in Mexico helping orphans is hardly a payback, but it's a start.

"When I was in high school," Donnetta continued, "my youth pastor's wife gave me a picture of Jesus with these words on the back: 'Only one life, will soon be passed. Only what's done for Christ will last.' I have always thought that was true, but I let my anger and confusion get in the way of acting like I did. Now that we have unpacked so much of my baggage, I want to live like I believe it."

"I think God is totally blessed by your attitude. He will give you the words to say when you need them. My old pastor used to say, 'God doesn't call the equipped. He equips the called.' The Lord proved that to me in the Philippines."

"Why were you there?" Donnetta questioned.

"To obey the Lord. The same reason you want to go to Mexico," I said. "I thought I was going to help other people, but God had some amazing lessons for me to learn." With Charlie sleeping serenely next to his mother, I started my story.

I have always been content to serve the Lord in my church nestled in the pine trees at the southern entrance to Yosemite National Park. (It's a tough job, but somebody's got to do it!) Despite the fact that my husband and I get many invitations to visit the mission field, we never felt led to go—not until Leslie, the head of our missions committee, came home from the Philippines.

Leslie is a sharp lady with a huge heart for God's people. She went to a Youth With a Mission base in Olongapo, Philippines, to help the workers as they ministered to former prostitutes. At the base, the girls were called "disciples," but on the streets, they were called "bar girls" because many of them were sold to bar owners by their own parents, who needed money to buy formula for their younger children. The girls went into prostitution because they wanted their families to have food, water, and medical care. As Leslie shared this story with us in our staff meeting, I found myself weeping. When she asked us to go with her, I was ready. She wanted to know if I would do a retreat for the "disciples." I couldn't wait!

As we got closer to the date we were to leave, it became obvious that my husband couldn't clear his schedule. I definitely preferred going with Bruce. But even though he couldn't go, I still felt led to be part of the team. When Leslie told the base leaders that I would do a retreat for the girls, they shared how weary they were and asked, "Could Linda do a retreat for us too?"

"I'd consider it an honor," I said.

The missionaries at the base were helpful and accommodating. Their sacrifice and commitment to God were a blessing to behold. But as the day for the retreat approached, I realized that they needed more than just encouragement. They needed tools to help them structure their roles more effectively. They needed insights into practical leadership techniques.

I forgot everything I had learned about being Mary and trusting God. I kicked into Martha mode and whined. *This is a tough one, Lord. These folks need real help. This is going to take more than three points and a poem!* I prayed in the privacy of my little room. *Why couldn't you have cleared Bruce's schedule? He can do leadership training in his sleep. How come you didn't send Ron George, the head of our board? He makes a living teaching people how to lead. Lord, you know I've got nothing to offer these people, and they deserve so much!* I lay awake with jetlag and concern.

The day of the retreat arrived and a neighboring pastor offered to take our team for some much needed rest and recreation. "I need to stay behind and get ready for the retreat," I told the team. I was really looking forward to a time of quiet so I could hear from God and find out what I was supposed to say to these road-weary servants. But nothing came.

Even as we boarded the jeepnee (a jeep from World War II that had been retrofitted and used as public transportation), I still had no idea what I was going to share. As a Martha personality, I need to have every talk memorized, every scripture selected, and every note written down in size fourteen font days ahead of time. I was trying not to panic as we rode across the city.

We settled into our rooms and wandered over to the meeting hall together. As I stood up and walked to the podium, I felt the eyes of expectation on me. The moment I opened my mouth, I heard the Lord clearly say in my mind, *Do temperaments.*

OK Lord, I can do that. I even brought along some tests because I always carry some in my speaking folder. That's a good idea, Lord.

Right away I sent someone to make copies. I questioned quietly, *How Lord? There are two Norwegian missionaries in the room, a bunch of Filipinos, I'm speaking in English, and the temperament terms are Greek. How is this supposed to work?*

I immediately thought of Gary Smalley and John Trent's use of animals to represent the different emotional temperaments. *That could work*, I reasoned. Then I remembered a conversation from the night before. I had eaten dinner with one of the Norwegians. We talked about how much we love our dogs, a sentiment not shared in Asia. I told Hilde that my dog chases away the skunks and coyotes. She had never seen a coyote, and she didn't know what a skunk was.

OK, Lord, so the animal idea is out.

At that moment I seemed to hear the Lord say, *Use Bible characters.*

Brilliant, I thought. *That's something we all have in common.* With a quick mental inventory, I realized that Simon Peter was a sanguine, the apostle Paul was clearly choleric, Elijah the prophet illustrates the melancholy temperament, and Abraham displayed phlegmatic personality traits. *Thanks, Lord. This will work.*

After I described each temperament and the team members took the test, I asked them to share what they found out about themselves. As the second person started to share, I clearly heard the Lord say, *Write this down.*

While the third team member was sharing, I looked down at what I had written and the presentation crystallized. I said to myself, *I can see it now. I know how to help these people.*

As they revealed their temperaments, it was clear what role each type of person needed to play at the base. They could operate in their strengths, function more efficiently, and be happier doing it. *God, you are so faithful*, I thought as I explained all of this to them slowly in English so that I wouldn't have to use a translator.

For the rest of the retreat, we reviewed their respective duties and responsibilities. We discussed spiritual self-care so that they would be able to stay in the battle. We talked about their dreams for the future of the organization. For years, I had sat with my husband through countless church leadership seminars. While I found them interesting, I'd often wondered why I was there. Now the Lord reminded me of all I had learned so that I could share it with his servants on that retreat. Without my even knowing it, God had prepared me for this retreat. My former pastor was right: God doesn't call the equipped; he equips the called.

"That's awesome," Donnetta Jean remarked.

"It was one of the most amazing things I've ever experienced," I agreed. "Girl, all you have to do is say yes to the Lord and he will do the rest. He will give you the words when you need them. I'm proof of that and so is the Bible. As Jesus sent out the disciples, he told them, 'Don't worry about what to say and how to say it. At that time you will be given what to say, for it will not be you speaking, but the Spirit of your father speaking through you' (Matt 10:19–20).

"The Lord has already poured into you what those folks in Mexico need. I can't wait to see what he's going to do through you. He doesn't want our ability; he wants our availability."

"So you think I'm ready to do something like this?" Donnetta questioned.

"I can give you a loud Amen! on that one." Donnetta and I laughed.

Then I asked if I could pray for her to have courage and strength.

What is the Lord asking you to do? Teach a Sunday school class, help in junior church, volunteer in the church office, visit sick folks from your church—the list is endless. The harvest is ready, but the laborers are few. He has gifted each one of us, and when we use our gifts for his kingdom, we discover the most fulfilling experience we can have this side of heaven. We move from pain to praise when we fulfill his purpose for our lives. Try it and see.

Truster Reconstructor

Are you faithful to follow? Take a spiritual gifts test at church or online to determine where you're gifted. Make a list of jobs in the church you can do with your gifts. Talk to someone on your pastoral staff who can help you use those gifts for the kingdom.

epilogue
Praise: Chocolate Chip Muffins

"C*omo esta?"* I greeted Donnetta as she walked into my office.

"*Muy, muy, muy bien,"* she teased back.

"That means it was good, huh?"

"I can't wait to tell you all about it," she said. "We'll have more time since Charlie is at Grandma's playing with his cousins from Washington. They are only in town today."

"He's become quite popular these days."

"I'm glad he gets along so well with other kids. He's such a blessing."

"I prayed for you while you were gone. I want to hear about what God did."

"It was beyond amazing. You won't believe what happened."

"On the mission field? Try me," I grinned.

"We had a lady show up just after we got there. It was obvious that she was really hurting. She had traveled for a day and a half in pain because she'd heard we were coming. The car carrying the medicine hadn't arrived yet, so we all circled up and prayed for her not to feel any pain while the dentists treated her. We went around the circle praying. This poor woman couldn't understand us, but with every prayer she calmed down a little more. By the time we made it all the way around the circle, the woman had gone from feeling excruciating pain to resting as quietly as a kitten. The dentists pulled her tooth and she didn't peep! Linda, if

115

I hadn't seen it with my own eyes, I wouldn't believe it! There were so many things like happening the whole time we were there."

"God always comes through."

"He sure does!" Donnetta said, clearly on a roll. "Madeline and her husband Ty led the team. They are the neatest couple. They were always doing little things for each other and complimenting one another. She was really good with the kids, and he had great skills with adults on our team and at the orphanage. He let her operate in her strengths and even praised her for them in front of the entire group. I want a marriage like that.

"You would have been so proud of me, Linda. I spoke in front of everyone."

"What?" I exclaimed. "Tell me more."

"OK, but I'm going to use your gift of making a short story long," Donnetta teased. We chuckled. I loved seeing her enthusiasm.

"At the meeting just before we left, Madeline told us to prepare a testimony. She wanted us to have three or four sentences ready about what God had done in our lives. I pulled her aside after the meeting and told her she had no idea what she was asking me to do. She prayed for me, and all the way home I heard that scripture in Matthew over and over in my head, and I knew God would give me the words."

Donnetta continued her story with relish. "Every evening we had a chapel time with the kids at the orphanage. Ty had a different person from the team share a testimony each night. On Thursday night, he asked me to share my story. I couldn't believe how calm I was, but I knew the whole group was praying for me. I told the kids how hurt and angry I felt because my dad didn't want me. He wanted boys, not a girl, so I always felt rejected. But Jesus took care of that because he became my parent. He's never cruel, he promised to never leave us or forsake us, and he's always available anytime we need him. I even used the verse from Deuteronomy 31:8, 'The LORD himself goes before you and will be with you; he will never leave you nor forsake you. Do not be afraid; do not be discouraged.'"

"You're absolutely right. I am so proud!" I exclaimed.

"There was a twelve-year-old girl there named Angelina," Donnetta continued. "She spoke pretty good English, and I found myself thanking God I paid attention in the two years I took of high school Spanish. After I shared my testimony, she asked if she could talk to me. She opened up about the night her stepfather abused her. Her mother came in and found him hurting her, lost her cool, and shot and killed him. 'Mom's in prison, my abusive dad is dead, and I'm on my own,' she said with tears streaming from her big brown eyes.

"I told her, 'You're not alone, Angelina. The Lord is with you all the time. Jesus will be your daddy and pull you up in his lap when you need comfort just like he did for me.'

"Then I shared with her about the Daily Dialogue so she could feel connected to Christ all day long. After we talked, she let Madeline and me pray for her to let go and forgive her step-dad.

"Linda, I knew how to help Angelina because of my own recovery."

"Donnetta Jean, you're radiant. It warms my heart to see you so fulfilled! You glow, girl!" We giggled together.

"I've never felt anything this cool. Knowing that something I said helped this struggling girl was such a rush. It feels awesome to be used by God."

"I believe that," I affirmed.

Donnetta continued, "I know I'll go back to Mexico. I can't invest that much right now. Charlie is my priority, of course. But I've developed missionary blood, I can tell."

"Donnetta, you've tasted what it feels like to let God flow through you. Nothing puts wind in our sails more than fulfilling the purpose for which we were created—being used to bring glory to God. He can use you anywhere now. You don't have to be in Mexico or halfway around the world. There are Angelinas in your backyard, and now you know what to say to them."

"Now I'm not afraid to talk to them," she said. "My missions team was such a supportive bunch. It was a safe place to learn how to speak in front of a group. They prayed for me and encouraged me. I feel like I made some lifelong friends.

"There was a lady who went with us named Lucille. Before she had kids, she was a dental assistant, so we talked shop a lot. She quit when she had kids, and now they're all grown except for a son in college. He was the one who talked her into going on the trip. He went on a mission trip to Costa Rica with his college and loved it. Lucille said her husband makes good money and really wants it to be used for the kingdom of God, so he encouraged her to go too. Who are these men who empower women?" Donnetta mused out loud.

"They are out there and you're finding them," I said.

"Thank God! Anyway, Lucille and I talked until two in the morning one night about how we grew up. Her mom was a drug addict and alcoholic, and she felt a lot of rejection from her mother like I did from my dad. She spent nearly a year in therapy to deal with her pain too.

"Lucille told me she had to distance herself from her mom in order to stay sane. When I told her that I fired my dad, she got a good laugh out of that. Her comment was, 'I never really called it that, but it's pretty much what I did with my mom. I survived all these years by distancing myself from her craziness. I could not be responsible for the job she did as a mother, but I was still responsible, with God's help, to be a good daughter. So I sent her Mother's Day, birthday, and Christmas cards each year with pictures of the kids. That's all I could handle because the chaos in the family made me crazy. I had to differentiate to stay sane. My counselor told me that I only have so much currency in my sanity account, and my mother cost too much money.'

"'How do you deal with what the Bible says about honoring your father and mother?' I asked her. Lucille gave me some great insight. I told her how I needed to journal Monumental Moments so I wouldn't forget the nuggets of truth that set me free. So she helped me with the details of her story as I wrote. She said it would help me remember as it helped her reflect."

Donnetta read Lucille's story from her journal.

Lucille spent her early years taking care of her mother. She and her brother Stephen, who was three years older, handled most everything—the meals, laundry, and even her younger siblings, Julie and Travis, when they came along.

"Travis and Julie's father was the only man my mother ever loved, even if he wouldn't marry her, and she told that to anyone who would listen. It became obvious to Stephen and me that mom treated the younger kids far differently than we were treated. Mom bought Travis a car when he was barely sixteen. He promptly wrecked it, and she went out and bought him another one. He wrecked that too. Julie never learned how to do life, because every time she made a mess of things, mom came along with a broom to sweep it up. Julie was my only sister, and she started out so adorable. It broke my heart to watch her go down the tubes.

"I left home as soon as I could get out. My mom never forgave me. She sat at home smoking joints with Julie and writing me letters about what a rotten daughter I was. It took three months of therapy to realize that I couldn't fix it and another three months to understand that I wasn't a bad person.

"At my mom's funeral three years ago, I looked over at Stephen. He's a school teacher now, so handsome and polite. He loves his kids and is active in his church. Then I looked at Ted, my husband, standing beside our four beautiful children. By God's grace, I married an amazing man. He works so hard all day but still musters the energy to come home and involve himself with his family. He and I did a good job with our children.

"Then there was Julie in the corner seriously strung out on crank. She and mom had gotten into the harder stuff, and I think that contributed to mom's early death. Travis wasn't even there because he was doing time for possession of stolen property.

"As I stood by my mother's coffin, I had a lightning-bolt revelation from the Lord. What is it that we as parents want more than anything for our kids? We want them to grow up to be God-fearing, law-abiding, tax-paying citizens who take care of their families and live happy productive lives. In fact, that would honor us more than anything else they could do. I realized as we stood there that Stephen and I had done that. We brought honor to Mom, but only because we were able to distance ourselves from her. If we had stayed close to home and continued the dysfunctional dance that Mom wanted, like Julie and Travis did, that would not have happened."

Donnetta closed her journal. "Linda, I believe that God brought Lucille into my life to give me that information."

"And I am convinced that he will continue to bring people into your life when you need them, because—"

"God's got my back!" Donnetta interrupted. We both laughed.

"You have learned so much and come so far in your healing process. You're a different person from the cowering waif who sat on my couch a few months ago. Do you feel like you're a different person?" I asked, wanting her to reflect on all the changes she had recently demonstrated.

Donnetta Jean paused to ponder before she responded. "I feel that for the first time in my life, I live in the moment. I'm not fretting over the past or worrying about the future. That's all in the Lord's hands. I have today, and I'm walking through it with him. It's easier to do because I like myself now. I feel like I have something to offer."

"I'll say you do!" I agreed.

"Linda, I needed to get away from my dad, so I came here to find the confidence to earn a living. What I got instead was a life!"

"That is profound," I encouraged. "You've mastered so many of the skills you need to live a happy, healthy life. And while I don't have a diploma for you, I do have this." From the top of my file cabinet, I pulled a plate of chocolate chip muffins with a candle in each one. Setting them in front of her, I asked, "Do you remember the conversation about muffins that we had when we first met? You accused God of withholding the chocolate chip muffins you asked for and instead giving you zucchini muffins because they're good for you."

Donnetta chuckled. I put one of the muffins on a small plate and handed it to her.

"I can't believe you remember that," she mused. "I had such an attitude. How could you stand me?"

"You are authentic and determined. What's not to like?"

Donnetta grew pensive, "Linda, thank you for caring about me before I could care about myself. More than anything, I want to thank you for showing me how much God cares about me. It's changed my life.

"Before I came here, I thought I would carry my pain around forever. But now I feel like it's been turned into praise. God just keeps giving me chocolate chip muffins!" Donnetta Jean beamed as we spent the rest of our time together munching muffins and marveling at God's goodness.

Nearly a year and a half after our last meeting, I received an invitation in the mail to Donnetta Jean's wedding. She was marrying Madeline's step-nephew, an awesome guy with a beautiful eight-year-old daughter, who, according to Donnetta's letter, adores Charlie. "I found a great husband, a terrific dad for Charlie, a darling daughter, and Ty and Madeline as my extended family. God really does have my back!"

Truster Reconstuctor

Make praise a part of each day. Spend the first fifteen minutes of each praise session thanking God for his provision in your life—over a cup of coffee, in the shower, on your way to work, on your break. Make the time. Look for things each day to add to your Blessed List.